EYEWITNESS ◉ GUIDES

WEATHER

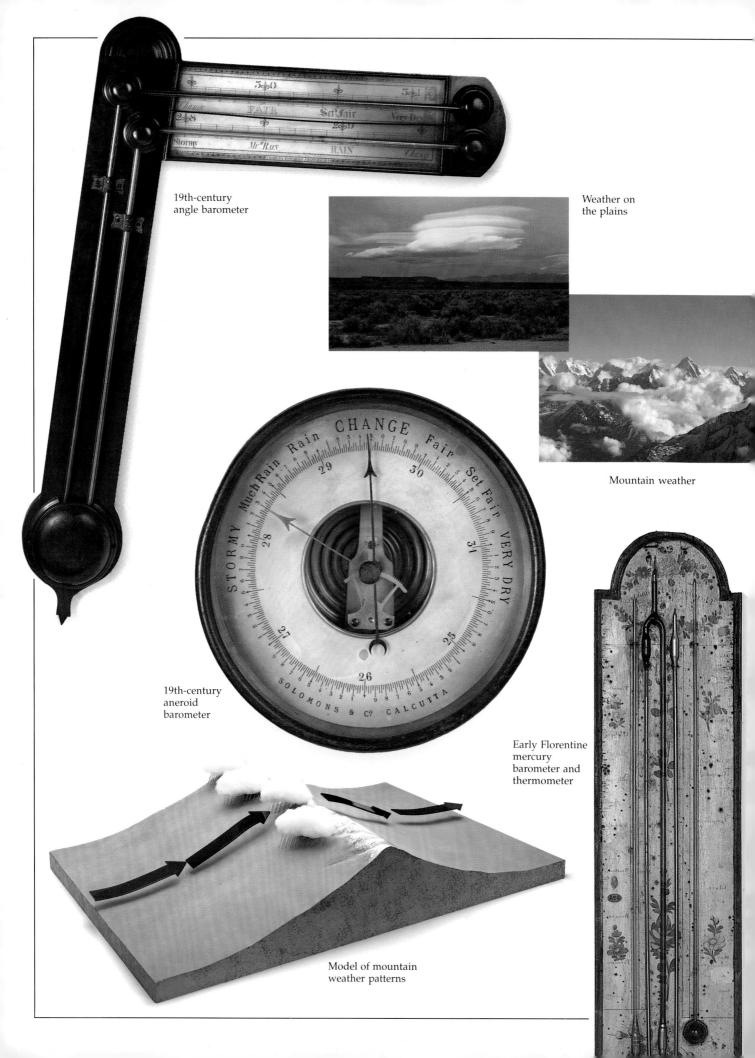

19th-century
angle barometer

Weather on
the plains

Mountain weather

19th-century
aneroid
barometer

Early Florentine
mercury
barometer and
thermometer

Model of mountain
weather patterns

Macrophotograph
of a snow crystal

EYEWITNESS ⦿ GUIDES

WEATHER

Written by
BRIAN COSGROVE

Pocket hygrometer

Weather cock

Early English
thermometer

Model of a
cold front

DK

DORLING KINDERSLEY
LONDON • NEW YORK • SYDNEY • MOSCOW
www.dk.com

Statue of an
Aztec sun god

Open and shut pinecones, indicating
damp or dry weather

Quadrant

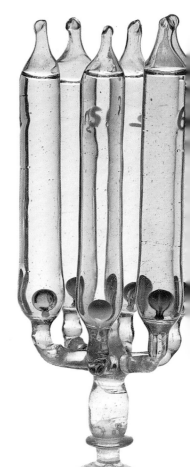

DK

A DORLING KINDERSLEY BOOK
www.dk.com

Project editors John Farndon, Marion Dent
Art editor Alison Anholt-White
Senior editor Helen Parker
Senior art editors Jacquie Gulliver, Julia Harris
Production Louise Barratt
Picture research Diana Morris
Special photography Karl Shone, Keith Percival
Editorial consultant Jim Sharp

This Eyewitness ® Guide has been
conceived by Dorling Kindersley Limited
and Editions Gallimard

First published in Great Britain in 1991
by Dorling Kindersley Limited,
9 Henrietta Street, London, WC2E 8PS

8 10 9

A CIP catalogue record for this book is available from
the British Library

ISBN 0-86318-578-9

Colour reproduction by Colourscan, Singapore
Typeset by Windsorgraphics, Ringwood, Hampshire
Printed in China by Toppan Printing Co., (Shenzhen) Ltd.

Early Florentine
glass thermometer

A Fitzroy
barometer

Contents

Orrery from the 18th century showing the motion of the planets and the seasons

The restless air

OUR PLANET IS SURROUNDED by a blanket of gases called the atmosphere. If it were not for the atmosphere we would not be able to live – we would be burned by the intense heat of the sun in the day or frozen by the icy chill of night. Look into the sky on a clear day, and you can see the atmosphere stretching some 1,000 km (600 miles) above you. Perhaps 99 per cent of it is as calm and unchanging as space beyond. But the very lowest 10 km (6 miles) – the air in which we live and breathe – is forever on the move, boiling and bubbling in the sun's heat like a vast cauldron on a fire. It is the constant swirling and stirring of this lowest layer of the atmosphere, called the troposphere, which gives us everything we call weather, from the warm, still days of summer to the wildest storms of winter.

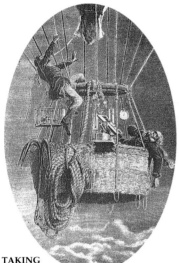

TAKING THE AIR
James Glaisher and Robert Coxwell were just two of many brave researchers who, in the 19th century, risked their lives in balloons to find out about the atmosphere. They found that the air got colder the higher they went. By 1902, though, unmanned balloons proved it got colder with height only up to a certain point called the tropopause, or the top of the troposphere.

BREATH FOR LIFE
The nature of air intrigued scientists for centuries. Then in the 1770s, Joseph Priestley's experiments with mice showed that air contains something that animals need to live. Like many, he thought this was a substance called phlogiston.

Whirls of cloud show the depressions that bring much bad weather to the mid-latitudes (pp. 32–35)

Belt of rain swept in by a depression

Dry, clear air over the Sahara desert

Clouds aligned with the steady northeasterly trade winds blowing towards the equator

Bank of cloud along the equator, marking the zone where the north and south trade winds meet

Europe

Africa

PLANET OF CLOUDS
In photographs from space, great swirls of cloud can be seen enveloping the Earth. These swirls dramatically highlight the constant motion of gases in the troposphere that gives us all our weather. Many of the world's major weather patterns can be seen clearly. Along the equator, for instance, is a ribbon of cloud thousands of kilometres long, formed because the intense heat of the sun here stirs up strong updraughts. These carry moisture from the ocean so high into the air that it cools and condenses to form clouds (pp. 24-25).

Whirls of cloud around mid-latitude depressions

Atlantic Ocean

Zone where unpredictable westerly winds blow

WHAT IS AIR
In the 1780s, French chemist Antoine Lavoisier found that Priestley's vital something was a gas which he called oxygen. He also found that air contained two other gases – nitrogen and carbon dioxide. Later, air was found to be roughly 21% oxygen, 78% nitrogen, and less than 1% carbon dioxide and other gases.

WORLD OF WEATHER

Some weather systems stretch right around the world, and on the far side of the globe, many similar cloud patterns can be seen. The equatorial cloud band is not so clear. But in the mid-latitudes, whirls of storm-bringing depressions sweeping westwards are clearly visible. The whirls occur because the turning of the Earth (from left to right, from west to east) spins the winds flowing between the equator and the poles – an effect called the Coriolis Effect (pp. 42–43). Notice how the whirls in the southern half of the globe turn in the opposite direction to those in the north.

Unpredictable westerly winds

North America

Band of cloud along the equator, caused by the strong, rising air currents stirred up by the hot sun here

Hurricanes spiralling across the Atlantic and into the Caribbean

South America

Clouds forming over warm ocean

Pacific Ocean

Depressions tracking across the Southern Ocean without hitting land before Australia

Thermosphere

Mesopause

Mesosphere

Stratopause

Stratosphere

Tropopause
Troposphere

Sea level

Height in km

HOT AND COLD AIR

As you go up through the atmosphere, the air becomes hotter or colder according to the layer. In the troposphere, the lowest layer where all weather occurs, the temperature drops steadily with height, a phenomenon called the lapse rate. Right up in the thermosphere, however, the sun can boost temperatures to 2000°C (3600°F).

ABOVE THE WEATHER

Weather only occurs in the troposphere, because this layer contains the most water vapour. Without water vapour, there would be no clouds, no rain or snow – and no weather. Flying through the troposphere can give a very bumpy ride. Modern jet airliners get around this problem by flying above the clouds in the stratosphere, where the air is still and clear.

Natural signs

Sᴀɪʟᴏʀꜱ, ꜰᴀʀᴍᴇʀꜱ, ᴀɴᴅ ᴏᴛʜᴇʀꜱ whose livelihood depends on the weather learned long ago that the world around them gave all kinds of clues to the weather to come – as long as they knew what to look for. Age-old advice passed down from generation to generation is offered on anything from the colour of the sky to the feel of your boots in the morning. Of course, some country weather lore is little more than superstition and all but useless for weather forecasting. But much is based on close observation of the natural world and can give an accurate prediction of the weather. Tiny variations in the air, which we cannot feel, often affect plants and animals. A change in their appearance or behaviour can be the sign of a change in the weather.

WHAT'S THE WEATHER LIKE?
Everyone – from travellers to sailors – had to know about the weather and be aware of natural signs around them.

NOTHING BUT A GROUNDHOG *above*
In the USA, 2 February is Groundhog Day. People say that if you can see a groundhog's shadow at noon on this day, the weather will be cold for six weeks. Sadly, weather records have proved the groundhog wrong many times.

SUN DAY OPENING
The scarlet pimpernel is often known as the "poo man's weather glass". It tiny flowers open wide sunny weather, but clos up tightly when rain is i the air.

Sunset

Sunrise

SEEING RED
Old country wisdom says: *Red sky at nig Shepherd's delight; Red sky in the morning, Shepherd's warning* – which means a fiery sunset should be followed by a fine morning, and a fiery dawn by storms. Weather experts are doubtful.

WEATHER WEED
People near the sea often hang out strands of kelp, for seaweed is one of the best natural weather forecasters. In fine weather, the kelp shrivels and is dry to the touch. If rain (pp. 30–31) threatens, the weed swells and feels damp.

CURLY WARNING
Wool is very responsive to the humidity, or moistness, of the air. When the air is dry, it shrinks and curls up. If rain is on its way, the air is moist, and the wool swells and straightens out.

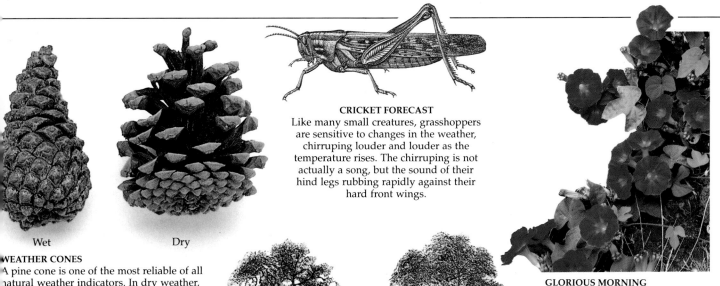

Wet   Dry

CRICKET FORECAST
Like many small creatures, grasshoppers are sensitive to changes in the weather, chirruping louder and louder as the temperature rises. The chirruping is not actually a song, but the sound of their hind legs rubbing rapidly against their hard front wings.

WEATHER CONES
A pine cone is one of the most reliable of all natural weather indicators. In dry weather, the scales on a pine cone open out; when they close up, it is a good sign that rain is on the way. This is because, in dry weather, the scales shrivel up and stand out stiffly. When the air is damp, they absorb moisture and become pliable again, allowing the cone to regain its normal shape.

Oak   Ash

GLORIOUS MORNING
Like the scarlet pimpernel, the petals of morning glory open and shut in response to weather conditions. These wide-open blooms indicate fine weather.

SOAK OR SPLASH?
According to some country weather lore, natural signs can indicate the weather for many days to come, as well as just the next few hours. An old English saying, for instance, is that: *If the oak flowers before the ash, we shall have a splash* (meaning only light rain for the next month or so). *If the ash flowers before the oak, we shall have a soak* (meaning very wet weather). There is little evidence to support any of these long-range predictions.

LYING COWS
When you can see cows lying down in a field, it is sometimes said that rain must be on the way. Apparently, the cows sense the dampness in the air and are making sure they have somewhere dry to lie. While many animals can indeed sense changes in the weather before humans, this particular prediction proves wrong as often as right.

SPRING IS HERE
Many natural signs are said to herald the end of winter, such as the first blooming of the white flowers of the horse chestnut tree. It is true that the flowers will only appear once the weather is mild enough – but this is no guarantee that there will be no more winter storms.

WINTER'S TAIL
Some country folk expect a severe winter if in autumn squirrels have very bushy tails, or gather big stores of nuts. Scientists have found no evidence to support this.

The science of weather

WEATHER AND THE ATMOSPHERE attracted the attention of thinkers and academics as long ago as the days of ancient Greece. However, the scientific study of weather, called meteorology, only began in Renaissance Italy in the 17th century, when instruments were developed to measure changes in the temperature of the air, its pressure, or weight, and its moisture content. It was in Italy, around 1600, that the great astronomer and mathematician Galileo Galilei made the first thermometer. Some 40 years later Galileo's first pupil Torricelli made the first practical barometer for measuring the pressure of the air. In the mid-17th century many gifted scientists and artists gathered under the patronage, or sponsorship, of Grand Duke Ferdinand II in the *Accademia del Cimento*, the Academy of Experiments in Florence, Italy. It was here at the Academy that they developed an array of sensitive instruments to make the first, planned, meteorological observations – paving the way for the scientific weather forecasts of today.

HEAT BALLS
Perhaps the first to prove that air expands when heated was Philo, a philosopher from the 2nd century B.C., who lived in Byzantium (now Istanbul in Turkey). When he connected a pipe from a hollow lead ball to a jug of water, air bubbled through the water when the ball was heated by the sun.

Water-absorbent paper discs

Pivot

Scale indicating humidity

WET OR DRY
In the 17th and 18th centuries people tried all kinds of ingenious ways of measuring the air's invisible moisture content. This simple hygrometer does just that. It is an English instrument dating from the early 18th century and consists of a balance with a pile of soft paper discs on one arm. If the air is dry, the discs dry out and weigh less. If the air is damp, they absorb water and weigh more, pulling the pointer up.

ICY WATER
This replica of one of the earliest, accurate hygrometers, designed by Grand Duke Ferdinand II in 1657, has a hollow core which can be filled with ice. Moisture in the air condenses on the outside and runs down into a measuring cylinder. The amount of water that is collected indicates the humidity of the air.

Flask for collecting water

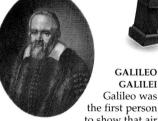

GALILEO GALILEI
Galileo was the first person to show that air has weight, and so paved the way for his pupil Torricelli's discovery of air pressure. Among Galileo's many discoveries were four satellites on the planet Jupiter, and the monthly and annual cycles of the moon.

WEATHER ACADEMY
The *Accademia del Cimento* in Florence became the focus of early scientific study of the atmosphere. This painting shows members of the academy in 1657, conducting an experiment on heat and cold. Using a thermometer, a mirror, and a bucket of ice, they are trying to find out if cold, like heat, can be reflected. It cannot.

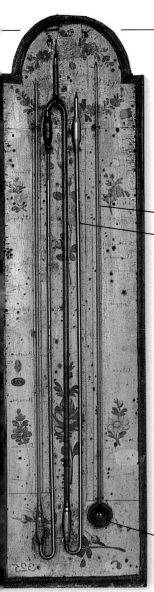

Thermometer

Barometer

Surface of water in tube

Needle indicating air pressure

EARLY WEATHER
The Italian script of this early 18th-century barometer shows how clearly people understood the barometer's value for forecasting weather.

Italian script describing expected weather

CROWN GLASS
Early Florentine meteorologists were served by the most skilled glass blowers in Europe, and it was their skill which made many of the earliest instruments possible. This elaborate and beautiful thermometer dates from shortly after the time of Galileo. Temperatures are registered by the rise and fall of coloured glass balls in the water contained in the tubes.

Balls made of coloured glass

Mercury reservoir

QUICKSILVER TUBE
Within 50 years of Torricelli's experiments with air pressure in the 1640s, barometers like this were in widespread use for measuring air pressure. Like Torricelli's original device, they worked by showing changes in the level of liquid quicksilver, or mercury, in a glass tube open to the air at the base. The level varies because when the air pressure is high, it weighs heavily on the mercury at the base, pushing it farther up the tube. When air pressure is low, the level of mercury drops.

EVANGELISTA TORRICELLI
In 1644, Torricelli made the first barometer, and proved the existence of air pressure. He filled a 1-m (3-ft) glass tube with mercury, then held the open end under the surface in a bowl of mercury. The mercury in the tube dropped to about 80 cm (32 in), leaving a vacuum at the top of the tube. Torricelli realized it was the weight, or pressure, of air on the mercury in the bowl that stopped it falling further.

Paper strip

DIAL HYGROMETER
The needle of this early hygrometer is made to move by a paper strip which shrinks or stretches in response to the dampness of the air.

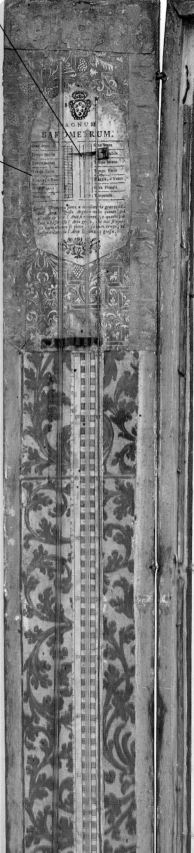

11

Watching the weather

MODERN WEATHER FORECASTING depends on gathering together and assessing millions of observations and measurements of atmospheric conditions, constantly recorded at the same time all over the world. No single system of measurements can give meteorologists a complete picture, so information is fed in from a wide range of sources. Most important are the many, land-based weather stations, from city centres to remote islands. Ships and radio signals from drifting weather buoys report details of conditions at sea. Balloons and specially equipped aeroplanes take measurements up through the atmosphere, while out in space weather satellites constantly circle the Earth, beaming back pictures of cloud and temperature patterns.

Modified Hercules transport plane

Tank containing equipment for recording holographic (3D) pictures of cloud particles

Wind vane for measuring wind direction

Thermometers in ventilated white surround

Radio transmitter for sending data via satellite to base

Temperature and humidity probes inside screen

Navigation light

Anemometer

Transmitter aerial

Barometric pressure sensor

STORM TOSSED
The need for ships to have advance warning of storms at sea encouraged people to set up organized weather forecasting networks.

Anemometer for measuring wind speed

Transmitter gives buoy position to orbiting satellite

FIXED STATION
At the heart of the world's weather watching is a network of about 10,000 permanent weather stations, linked together by the World Meteorological Organization. Reports from these stations are fed back every three hours (called "synoptic hours") by telephone to 13 centres around the world from Washington to Melbourne. This weather data is continuously passed on all around the world to countries who make up their own weather forecasts.

SEA WATCH
Since the 1970s, drifting weather buoys have been used to help fill in the gaps left by ships' observations about conditions at sea. They float freely with the ocean currents and transmit automatic readings back to land via satellites. These satellites can pinpoint where the buoy is to within 2 km (1 mile).

Solar panel to power navigation light

HIGH VIEW
Since 1957, satellite pictures have played a vital role in monitoring the weather. They provide two basic types of picture. Normal photographs show the Earth and clouds just as we would see them, while infrared pictures record infrared radiation to show temperatures at the nearest visible point.

OUT OF THIS WORLD
There are two types of weather satellite. Geostationary satellites always remain fixed in the same spot high above the equator, about 36,000 km (21,600 miles) out in space. There are five of them altogether, providing an almost complete picture of the globe (except for the two poles) every half hour. Polar-orbiting satellites circle the Earth in strips from pole to pole. They provide a continuously changing and more detailed weather picture from closer to the Earth's surface.

Tank containing high-powered pulsed laser for taking holographic pictures

Radar to give a clear picture of the clouds

Instruments mounted on a long nose to give temperature and humidity readings unaffected by the plane itself

SEPH HENRY
1848, Joseph Henry of the ithsonian Institution in USA, set up a system obtain simultaneous ather reports from oss the continent. 1849, over 200 servers were taking asurements nation- de and sending m back to Mr. Henry Washington. These re displayed on a large p in the Institution, and ovided daily weather reports the *Washington Evening Post*.

FLYING EYE
Specially-modified research aircraft are fitted with an array of sophisticated equipment to detect weather conditions at various levels in the atmosphere. In the USA, five different types of aircraft are used to monitor hurricanes, including some designed to fly right into the eye of the storm. This British plane (above and right) is designed to take a wide range of atmospheric weather measurements. Nicknamed "Snoopy" because of its long probing nose, it monitors the upper atmosphere in far more detail than by using balloons.

Underside of aircraft's wing capsule

SKY PROBE
At midnight and midday Greenwich Mean Time, hundreds of helium, gas-filled balloons are launched into the upper atmosphere all around the world. As they rise higher and higher, automatic instruments frequently take humidity, pressure, and temperature readings. These are transmitted back to the ground by instruments called radiosonde. Wind speed at various heights can be calculated by tracking the way the balloon rises.

Balloon is tracked either by radar or visually with survey equipment

Tube for filling balloon with helium gas

Long line for supporting recording instruments

TA COLLECTION
rucial advance in accurate weather forecasting s Samuel Morse's invention of the telegraph in 1840s. Complex messages were sent instantly r long distances through electric cables, by ping out a coded sequence of short and long ses, known as the Morse Code. Once a graph network was established, weather ervations were sent back to a central bureau, ing a complete picture of a continent's weather.

Forecasting

EXPERIENCED WEATHER WATCHERS still predict local weather using simple instruments and careful observations of the skies. Larger-scale forecasting – the kind that provides daily radio and television bulletins – is a much more sophisticated and complex process. Every minute of the day and night, weath observations taken by weather stations, ships, satellites, balloons, and radar al around the world are swapped by means of a special Global Telecommunications System, or GTS. At major forecasting centres, all this data is continuously fed into powerful supercomputers, able to carry out millions of calculations a second. Meteorologists use this information to make short-range weather forecasts for the next 24 hours, and draw up a special map, or "synoptic chart", indicating air pressure, wind, cloud cover, temperature, and humidity. Also they can make fairly accurate long-range forecasts for up to a week.

CHANGE OF AIR
French physicist Jean de Borda first showed that changes in air pressure are related to wind speed.

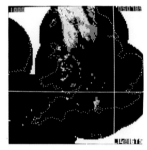

RAIN SCAN
Radar has proved invaluable in monitoring rainfall. Radar signals reflect any rain, hail, or snow within range, and the reflection's intensity shows how heavily rain is falling. Computer calculations then let meteorologists compile a map of rainfall intensity, as above.

HIGH DAYS
Fair weather, with blue skies and fluffy cumulus clouds (pp. 24–25), is often associated with high-pressure zones, or "anticyclones".

Spiked and bumped lines indicate occluded fronts, where cold fronts catch up with warm fronts and keep them off the ground (pp. 32–35)

Spiked lines indicate a cold front, where cold air is pushing under warm

BAROGRA
Many fixed weather stations equipped with a barograph to mak continuous record of changing air pressure. Like m barographs, this one is based around an aneroid barome Unlike mercury barometers (pp. 10–11), aner barometers have a drum, containing a vacuum sealed particular air pressure. As the air pressure changes, drum expands and contracts. In a barograph, a p attached to the lid of the drum draws the ups and dov continuously on a rotating sheet of graph pap

STORM BY SATELLITE
The cold front and depression, marked on the synoptic chart, are clearly revealed by the whirl of clouds in this satellite photograph, taken at exactly the same time as the chart represents.

Closely spaced isobars indicate strong wind

Low, or depression

DULL DAYS
Wet and stormy weather, with grey skies and high winds, is often associated with fronts and low-pressure zones, or depressions, sometimes known as cyclones (pp. 38–39).

CHARTING THE WEATHER
The most obvious features on any weather map, or synoptic chart, are the long, curving lines called isobars. These are lines linking points of equal pressure, usually measured in millibars (mb), and they provide a good indication of the likely weather. Inside circles linked by low-pressure isobars (typically 1000 mb, or below) are depressions, where the air pressure is low, because air is rising. These frequently bring wind, clouds, and rain (pp. 32–35). Inside circles linked by high-pressure isobars (1020 mb and over) are highs, where air is sinking. These usually give dry, settled weather (pp. 18–19). Weather charts like these are called "synoptic", which means "seen together". Ideally, all the observations used to compile the map would be synoptic – taken at exactly the same time – but this is rarely completely practical. So the weather computer must be programmed to compensate for any differences in the observation time.

Weather stations, with observations for wind, cloud cover, and other factors (see key)

Ridge of high pressure

Bumped lines indicate a warm front, where warm air is pushing over cold

Isobars joining points of equal air pressure

WEATHER BY NUMBERS
Lewis Richardson first devised "numeric weather predictions" in the 1920s. He believed that the key to weather forecasting was to observe temperature, humidity, pressure, and wind simultaneously at evenly spaced points (gridpoints) throughout the world, at various fixed heights (levels) in the atmosphere. From these, he argued, future synoptic values could be calculated, and so weather could be predicted across a wide area. The calculations involved were immense, and Richardson tried with this purpose-built calculator. It is only with the development of super-computers, able to do billions of calculations quickly, that numeric forecasting has become possible.

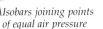

Key to symbols

Temperature: 7°C (45°F)

Current weather: continuous, heavy rain

Visibility: 2.5 km (1.5 miles)

Dew point: 6°C (43°F)

Stratus cloud

Cloud cover complete

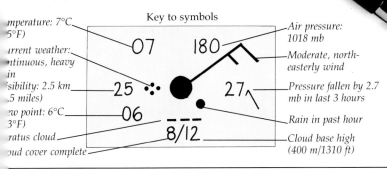

Air pressure: 1018 mb

Moderate, north-easterly wind

Pressure fallen by 2.7 mb in last 3 hours

Rain in past hour

Cloud base high (400 m/1310 ft)

A closeup view of the sun, showing a violent storm erupting at the surface

The power of the sun

WITHOUT THE SUN, there would be no weather. Light from the sun is the energy which fuels the world's great weather machine. Sunshine, wind, rain, fog, snow, hail, thunder – every type of weather happens because the heat of the sun keeps the atmosphere constantly in motion. But the power of the sun's rays to heat the air varies – across the world, through the day, and through the year. All these variations depend on the sun's height in the sky. When the sun is high in the sky, its rays strike the ground directly, and its heat is at a maximum. When it is low in the sky, the sun's rays strike the ground at an angle, and its heat is spread out over a wider area. It is largely because of these variations that we get hot weather and cold weather, hot places and cold places.

Gnomon

DAILY RHYTHMS *left and above*
The shadow cast by the sundial's needle, or "gnomon", shifts as the sun moves through the sky from sunrise to sunset, indicating the time of day. So too does the sun's power to heat the air vary through the day – with profound effects upon the weather we experience.

HOT SPOTS
Deserts occur wherever there is little moisture in the air. But the hottest deserts, like the Sahara, are in the tropics where the sun's power is at its greatest.

18th-century brass garden sundial

☐ Mountain
☐ Taiga: cold plains
☐ Polar

Temperate ☐
Mediterranean ☐
Savannah: warm plains ☐
Subtropical ☐
Tropical ☐
Hot desert ☐

Earth *Moon*

POLAR COLD
Vast areas of the Arctic and Antarctic, where it is always cold, are covered in a permanent sheet of ice, up to 300 m (985 ft) thick.

THE WORLD'S CLIMATES
Because the Earth's surface is curved, the sun's rays strike different parts at different angles, dividing the world into distinct climate zones, each with its own typical weather. (A place's climate is just its average weather.) The world's hottest places are in the tropics, straddling the equator, for here the sun is almost overhead at noon. The coldest places are at the poles, where even at noon, the sun is so low in the sky that its power is spread out over a wide area. In between these extremes lie the temperate zones. Within these broad zones, however, climates vary considerably according to such factors as proximity to oceans and mountains, and height above sea level.

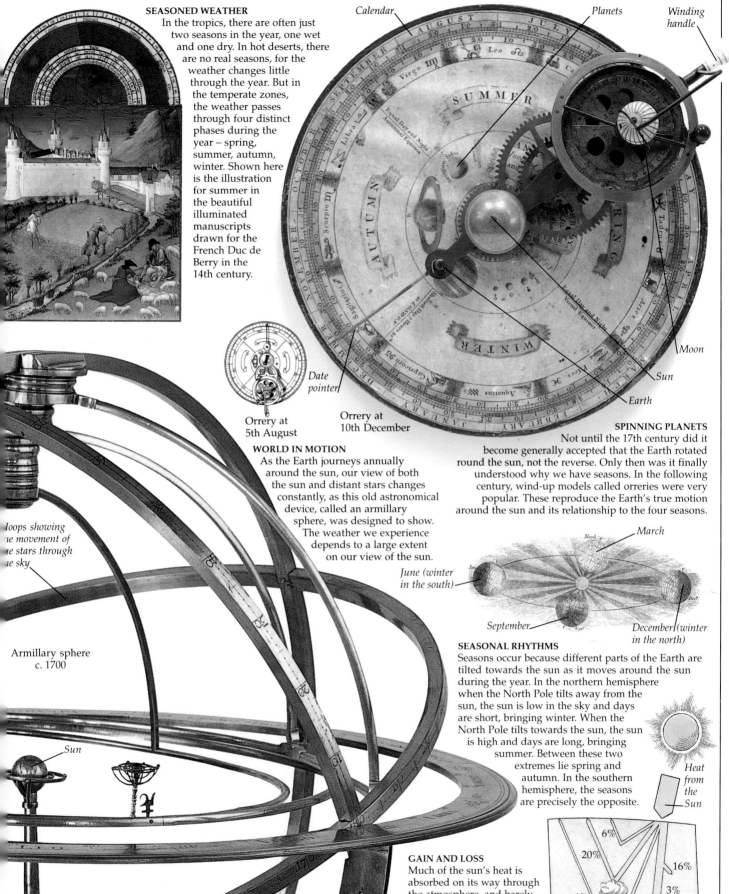

SEASONED WEATHER

In the tropics, there are often just two seasons in the year, one wet and one dry. In hot deserts, there are no real seasons, for the weather changes little through the year. But in the temperate zones, the weather passes through four distinct phases during the year – spring, summer, autumn, winter. Shown here is the illustration for summer in the beautiful illuminated manuscripts drawn for the French Duc de Berry in the 14th century.

Calendar

Planets

Winding handle

SUMMER

AUTUMN

WINTER

Moon

Sun

Earth

Date pointer

Orrery at 5th August

Orrery at 10th December

WORLD IN MOTION

As the Earth journeys annually around the sun, our view of both the sun and distant stars changes constantly, as this old astronomical device, called an armillary sphere, was designed to show. The weather we experience depends to a large extent on our view of the sun.

loops showing the movement of the stars through the sky

Armillary sphere c. 1700

Sun

SPINNING PLANETS

Not until the 17th century did it become generally accepted that the Earth rotated round the sun, not the reverse. Only then was it finally understood why we have seasons. In the following century, wind-up models called orreries were very popular. These reproduce the Earth's true motion around the sun and its relationship to the four seasons.

March

June (winter in the south)

September

December (winter in the north)

SEASONAL RHYTHMS

Seasons occur because different parts of the Earth are tilted towards the sun as it moves around the sun during the year. In the northern hemisphere when the North Pole tilts away from the sun, the sun is low in the sky and days are short, bringing winter. When the North Pole tilts towards the sun, the sun is high and days are long, bringing summer. Between these two extremes lie spring and autumn. In the southern hemisphere, the seasons are precisely the opposite.

Heat from the Sun

GAIN AND LOSS

Much of the sun's heat is absorbed on its way through the atmosphere, and barely half reaches the ground. But the Earth stays warm because the "greenhouse" gases in the air (pp. 60-61) keep most of the heat in.

6%

20%

16%

4%

3%

51%

A sunny day

OVER MUCH OF THE WORLD, sunny weather and almost cloudless skies are common, especially in summer. Indeed, in the eastern Sahara, the sun is covered by clouds for less than 100 hours of the year. Sunny weather is actually the most stable, persistent kind of weather, and a day that starts sunny and cloudless is likely to stay that way. Clouds form only when there is enough moisture in the air – and enough movement to carry the moisture high into the atmosphere. If the air is both dry and calm, clouds will not form, nor will they be blown in from elsewhere. This is why sunny weather is often associated with high atmospheric pressure (pp. 14–15), where the air is slowly sinking and virtually still. In summer, high pressure can persist for a long time – as the sinking air pushes out any new influences – and the weather remains warm and sunny for days on end.

The hottest place in the world is Dallol in Ethiopia, where annual temperatures average 34.4°C (94°F).

SUN GOD
So important was reliable sunshine in ancient times – not only for heat and light but for ripening crops – that many early civilizations worshipped the sun. The Aztecs of Mexico, in particular, built vast temples to the sun god Tonatuich, and made many bloody sacrifices, both animal and human, to persuade him to shine brightly on them.

GROWING LIGHT
Green plants need plenty of sunshine, for all their energy for growth comes directly from the sun. Cells in their leaves contain chlorophyll which converts sunlight into chemical energy by photosynthesis.

Image of sun reflected in glass orb

BURNING RECORD
Meteorologists usually record hours of sunshine on a simple device called a parheliometer, or Campbell Stokes sunshine recorder. This has a glass ball to focus the sun's rays on to a strip of card so that they burn the card. As the sun moves round during the day, so do the scorch marks on the paper, giving a complete scorch mark record of the day's sunshine. This early recorder (viewed from above) was made by the Irish physicist Sir George Stokes in 1881.

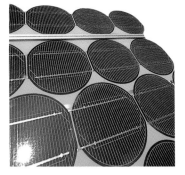

SOLAR POWER
Nearly all our energy comes from the sun. Solar cells let us tap this energy directly, using light-sensitive crystals to convert sunshine into electricity. Solar power is only practical in places where sunshine records are consistent.

Burn marks on card

1024 mb   Full sun   Light wind

BLUE SKY
In summer, sunny days tend to be hot, as there is little cloud in the way to block out the sun's rays – clouds can soak up more than 80% of the sun's heat on a cloudy day. But without clouds to trap heat rising from the ground, temperatures can often drop rapidly after sunset. Indeed, in winter, sunny weather usually brings foggy mornings and frosty nights. Clear, blue skies may look uninteresting at first sight, but there is often plenty going on, especially when the atmosphere is humid (pp. 50-51) or dusty.

Wisps of high cirrus cloud, made entirely of ice. These may be the remnants of a vanished storm cloud, since ice vapourizes more slowly than water. But they could signal the onset of a warm front (pp. 32-33)

Remnants of contrails

Contrails left in the wake of jet planes, especially in cold, dry air. Made of ice, like cirrus clouds, contrails form when the hot gases that shoot out behind the jet hit cool air and rise rapidly. As they rise, they expand and cool so sharply that water droplets soon condense and then freeze

Small, short-lived, fluffy cumulus clouds may be formed here and there by rising warm air currents

Low-level haze, especially over urban areas. Winds may be too light to disperse smoke and dust, and, if the pressure is high, a temperature inversion may trap water vapour and pollutants in a layer just above the ground (pp. 48-49)

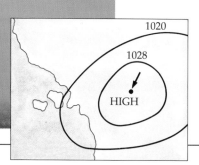

1020

1028

HIGH

Frost and ice

KEEPING THE COLD OUT
In some parts of the world, frosty nights are characterized by the malevolent, spiky "Jack Frost", who leaves his icy finger marks on every window pane.

WHEN A CALM, CLEAR, DRY NIGHT follows a cold winter's day, a sharp frost may well descend on many places by morning. Temperatures rarely climb high in winter, when the sun is low in the sky during the day, and the nights are long. If the night sky is clear, too, then any heat retained in the ground can flow away quickly, allowing temperatures to plummet. Frosts are rare but by no means unheard of in the tropics – and almost continuous towards the poles. In Vostok, in Antarctica, temperatures average a bitter -57.8°C (-72°F). In the mid-latitudes, frosts occur whenever the conditions are right, more often inland than near the coast, where the sea tends to retain heat longer.

The low temperatures near the ground that bring a frost can also create fog (pp. 48–49). The moisture condenses in the cold air and hangs there, because there is little wind to disperse it. If the fog coats things with ice, it is called freezing fog

Thick coating of rime, a white ice formed when an icy wind blows over leaves, branches, and other surfaces. Temperatures usually have to be lower for rime than for hoar frost

Hoar frost coats freezing cold surfaces such as soil and metal with ice crystals

ICING UP
High in the atmosphere, air temperatures are always below freezing, and the wings of high-flying aeroplanes can easily become coated with rime ice. This drastically affects their performance. Most jet airliners now have de-icing equipment.

COLD FRAME
Frost can create beautiful patterns of ice crystals. If the weather is especially severe, delicate traceries of "fern frost" may appear on the inside of windows. First, dew forms on the cold glass. Then, as some dewdrops cool below freezing point, they turn into ice crystals, encouraging more ice crystals to form.

HOAR THORNS
When water vapour touches a very cold surface, it can freeze instantly, leaving spiky needles of "hoar frost" on leaves and branches – and also on cars, for their metal bodies get very cold. Hoar frost tends to occur when the air temperature is around 0°C (32°F), and the ground is much colder – but the air must be moist to create the ice crystals.

FROZEN ARCH
Arctic and Antarctic temperatures are perpetua below freezing, and ice can last hundreds of yea Sometimes vast chunks of ice, or icebergs, break off polar glaciers and float out to sea. They float because water becomes less dense when it freez but most of their bulk lies below the water.

Even though there is a mist near the ground, the sky above is clear, allowing heat to escape during the night

Frost is white because the crystals contain air

ICY COATING (above)

When the conditions are cold enough, moisture from the air freezes, leaving the ground, leaves, branches, and many other surfaces coated with a thin layer of ice crystals, although sometimes frost can occur because heat is radiated from the ground on clear nights. Spring and autumn frosts often happen this way. In mid-winter, though, a chill polar wind may be enough to bring frost.

ICE HOUSE

Very low temperatures can produce spectacular ice effects. Most icicles form when cold nights freeze drips of melting snow. This house in Chicago, USA, got its remarkable coat of ice when firemen turned their hoses on it to put out a fire – on the coldest night in the city's history, when temperatures plummeted to -32°C (-26°F) on 10th January 1982.

MARKET ON ICE

In the early 1800s, the weather tended to be much colder than today. Frosts could be so hard that even the River Thames in London froze solid. The last "frost fair" held on the ice was in 1814, before the weather began to warm up.

Water in the air

EVEN ON THE SUNNIEST DAY, the horizon often shimmers indistinctly in a haze, and distant hills look soft and grey. Some haze is dust and pollution, but most is simply moisture in the air. Even over the hottest deserts, the atmosphere is literally full of water. Like a dry sponge, the air continually soaks up water that evaporates from oceans, lakes, and rivers, and transpires (sweats) from trees, grass, and other plants. Most of the moisture is water vapour, a gas mixed almost invisibly into the air. When it cools enough, the moisture condenses into tiny droplets of water, forming the clouds, mist, and haze that continually girdle the Earth. Water vapour will form water droplets only if the air contains plenty of dust, smoke, and salt particles, called condensation nuclei, for it to condense on to. If the air is very pure, there will not be enough nuclei, so clouds and mist will not form.

DEW DROPS
Moisture condenses as air cools because the cooler the air is, the less water vapour it can hold. So as it cools down, air becomes nearer saturation – that is, the limit it can hold. Once it reaches this limit, called the dew point, water vapour condenses into droplets. After a cold night, dew drops can be seen sparkling on grass and spiders' webs.

Scale shows humidity

Human hair stretches in moist air and contracts in dry air

Hair hygrometer

WET HAIR
The moisture content of the air, called humidity, can be measured using a hair hygrometer. Meteorologists need to know how much water there is in the air, in proportion to the most water it can hold at that temperature and pressure. This is called relative humidity.

When the water level in the spout is high, pressure is low, and storms can be expected

Closed glass bulb

When working, the level of water in the weather glass would have been much higher

STORM GLASS
Like mercury in barometer, water levels can be used to monitor air pressure. Though not accurate, "weather glasses" like this were cheaper to make than proper mercury barometers, and were quite common on small boats.

WEATHER HOUSE
Before weather forecasting was common, weather houses like this used to be popular. Actually, they are hair hygrometers. When the air is moist, a hair inside the house stretches and lets the man come out of the door. If the air is dry, the hair shrinks, pulling the man in and letting the woman pop out.

Gruß aus Villach

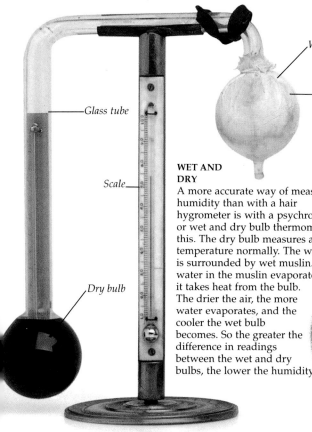

Wet bulb

Damp muslin cover

Glass tube

Scale

Dry bulb

WET AND DRY

A more accurate way of measuring humidity than with a hair hygrometer is with a psychrometer, or wet and dry bulb thermometer like this. The dry bulb measures air temperature normally. The wet bulb is surrounded by wet muslin. As water in the muslin evaporates, it takes heat from the bulb. The drier the air, the more water evaporates, and the cooler the wet bulb becomes. So the greater the difference in readings between the wet and dry bulbs, the lower the humidity.

SMALL MEASURES

This tiny pocket hygrometer – less than 4 cm (1 $\frac{3}{5}$ in) in diameter – uses human hair to work the needle and is surprisingly accurate. Instruments like this used to be very popular with walkers, who wanted to predict a shower.

MISTY MOUNTAINS

At night, the ground cools down gradually, and so cools the air above it. If the air temperature drops below its dew point, it becomes saturated, and water droplets condense into the air to form a mist. In mountain areas (pp. 52–53), mist will often gather in the valleys in the morning because cold air flows downhill in the night, and settles there.

Raindrop just large enough to overcome tension

Small raindrops held on glass by surface tension

GROWING RAINDROPS

When rain falls on a window, only the biggest drops run down the pane. Unless a raindrop is big to start with, a phenomenon known as surface tension will hold it on the glass until another drop falls in the same place. Then the tension will be broken, and the drops will run down the pane in rivulets. In the same way, tiny droplets of water in a cloud will only start to fall as rain once they are large and heavy enough to over-come air resistance.

...ATER
...SION

...t were not for the moisture in the air, we could nearly
...ays see into the distance much more clearly. Fog and
...t cut down visibility dramatically, but even on
...parently clear days, there is often a slight haze in the
..., making distant hills look pale and indistinct.

DAMP TRADE

Many activities, such as silk-making in China, depend upon the humidity of the air. If the air is not damp enough, the caterpillars will not spin the thread properly.

Rivulet gathering in other drops on its path

The birth of a cloud

Look into the sky on a fine day, when fleecy, "cotton wool" clouds are scudding overhead. Watch carefully for a while and you will see the clouds constantly changing in shape and size. Every so often, new clouds appear out of the blue, curling and growing like spun candyfloss. Others shrink and vanish into nothing, especially late in the day as the air grows cooler. Short-lived clouds like these, called cumulus, or "heap" clouds, form because the sun heats the ground unevenly. In some places this creates bubbles of warm air that drift upwards through the cooler air around. As they rise, the bubbles cool, until, high in the air, water vapour condenses to form a cloud. Bubbles, or convection cells, like these rarely last for more than 20 minutes. Often, half a dozen new cells bubble up in the same place and the resulting cloud can last for an hour or so. A few clouds may build up so much that an isolated shower of rain will fall. Occasionally, when the air is moist and the sun hot, fleecy cumulus clouds grow enough to create their own internal air currents, and then something more ominous starts to happen. The cloud billows higher into the atmosphere, and may turn into a huge thundercloud, lasting for about nine hours, before releasing its large load of moisture in a terrific downpour (pp. 36–37).

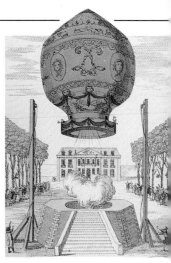

HOT AIR
As air heats up, it expands and becomes lighter than the cool air around, and so it rises. The Montgolfier brothers exploited this when they filled a balloon with hot air heated by a fire in a cauldron beneath it to make the first-ever manned flight over Paris in l783.

STEAM CLOUDS
Clouds form in the sky in much the same way that clouds of steam billow from a steam engine's funnel. As hot, moist air escapes from the funnel, it expands and becomes cooler, until it is so cold that any moisture condenses into tiny water droplets. So a bubble of rising, warm air expands and cools until water vapour condenses to form clouds.

Early clouds often disappear, evaporating into the drier surrounding air

In the morning, when the thermals are weak, small individual clouds are formed, with clear sky between them

2 NEW BUBBLES
The same areas of the ground often remain hottest during the day, so warm air continues to bubble up in the same places. Sometimes, the clouds formed by these bubbles will drift away on the wind, and another will take its place, creating "streets", or lines, of clouds for many miles downwind.

1 SMALL BEGINNINGS
It takes some time for the sun to heat the ground, so the first clouds are very small.

Clouds often lean downwind, because the air is moving faster at higher levels than lower down towards the surface

3 BUILDING CLOUDS
Clouds will evaporate and disappear only if the surrounding air is dry, so any increase in moisture means that they evaporate more slowly. They will last longer as the day goes by, because rising air will continue to bring in new moisture.

Thermals

Bubbles of warm air, or thermals, form over hot spots on the ground, such as an airport. Because the bubble is warmer it expands, becoming less dense than the surrounding air. Drifting up into the sky, it expands further as air becomes thinner and pressure drops. As it expands, it cools down until at a certain height – the condensation level – it is so cool that the moisture it contains condenses out

ELK'S BREATH

The warm, moist breath of a mammal is normally invisible – unless the air is so cold that moisture in its breath condenses into droplets and then turns into tiny clouds.

A thick cloud has a very dark base, because no light passes through the cloud from above

5 HIGH FLIERS

The movement of air inside cumulus clouds often becomes organized into "cells", with strong updraughts and downdraughts quite close to one another. Pilots try to avoid flying through large cumulus clouds, because the sudden changes between rising and falling air cause a very bumpy ride, and passengers have to wear seatbelts. The cloud that is shown in these pictures has now grown very large. If it grew even larger, some of the water vapour might turn to ice, which would start the formation of raindrops.

Clouds appear brilliantly white in sunshine, because the tiny water droplets reflect light extremely well

4 UP, UP, AND AWAY

As the day heats up, more thermals drift up from the surface. One may arrive so close behind another that a single cloud is created. Moist air around the first thermal helps the second to grow higher before it too starts to decay. Each cloud contains several thermals at different stages of development.

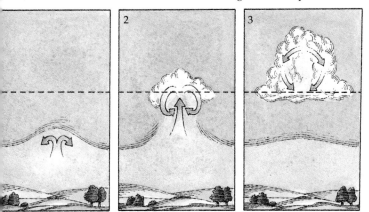

CLOUD FORMS

Clouds form whenever there is enough moisture in the air, and whenever moist air is lifted high enough into the air to cool and condense (1). On a clear day, the sun heats the ground, sending up bubbles of rising warm air wherever the ground heats most (2). Fleecy cumulus clouds will appear in the sky and disappear when these bubbles no longer form (3).

ARTIFICIAL CLOUDS

Not all clouds are natural ones. Inside power-station cooling towers, the large quantities of water at a low temperature produce enormous volumes of very moist, slightly warm air, which often condenses immediately above the towers into low, "artificial" cumulus clouds.

A cloudy day

CLOUDY SKIES ARE RARE OVER DRY DESERTS. But in more humid areas, the weather may stay dull and overcast for days on end. Sometimes, fluffy, short-lived cumulus clouds (pp. 28–29) heap up enough to form a dense bank, shutting out the sun. More often, though, persistently cloudy skies are associated with layered, or "stratus", clouds. Clouds like these build up gradually over a wide area when a warm, moist wind meets colder air. As this warm air rides slowly up over cold air, moisture steadily condenses from the air as it cools – creating a vast blanket of cloud that can be several hundred metres thick and stretch for hundreds of kilometres.

MEASURING CLOUD HEIGHT
The Victorians calculated the height of clouds by using cameras and giant tripods, but meteorologists nowadays use laser beams pointed at the base of the cloud to judge its height. Cloud cover, however, is worked out visually, by estimating roughly what proportion of the sky is obscured by the cloud directly overhead – usually in quarters.

THREE KINDS OF CLOUD
On some cloudy days, nothing but a thin blanket of low stratus is visible. On other days, many kinds of clouds may be seen at different heights in the sky. Thin sheets of stratus may not be enough to stop warm updraughts of air, or thermals, developing and cumulus clouds growing (pp. 24–25), especially if the sun is strong. In this picture, taken near mountains close to a weak cold front (pp. 34–35), there are not only stratus and cumulus, but also a third type, called lenticular clouds, formed by waves in the wind in the lee of mountains (pp. 54–55).

Small cumulus clouds are unlikely to give much rain – although there might be light showers later in the day

Stratus cloud

Thermals (pp. 24–25) rising beneath cumulus clouds

UPS AND DOWNS
Cumulus clouds indicate to glider pilots the presence of updraughts, or thermals, that they need for climbing. These are common over ploughed fields and other warm areas of soil, but over comparatively cold bodies of water, such as lakes, the thermals will not form, and gliders sink back down towards the ground. The same thing happens if thick layers of medium-height or high cloud cover the sky and cut off the warmth of the sunlight from the ground

*Medium-height altocumulus
and altostratus clouds*

1000 mb   Full cloud   Wind
            cover   moderate

*Cloud cover is extensive,
but there are still patches
of blue sky visible*

*When there are several layers
of humid air, wave-clouds (or
lenticular clouds, pp. 54–55)
appear to be stacked on top of
one another like a pile of plates*

*Wave-clouds stay in
the same place until
conditions change*

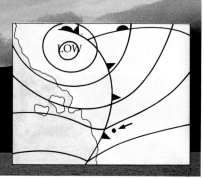

*Good visibility in the clear
air beneath the clouds*

SMOOTH OR LUMPY
In *The Beauty of the Heavens*
(London, 1845), the
Victorian painter Charles F.
Blunt depicted two main
groups of clouds: cumulus
(detail, left), which are
heaped clouds formed by
the rise of individual
bubbles of air (pp. 24–25);
and cirrostratus (detail,
right), where whole layers
of air are forced to rise, for
example at a front (pp.
32–33), forming widespread
sheets of cloud.

Clouds of all kinds

CLOUDS FLOAT ACROSS THE SKY in all sorts of shapes, sizes, and colours, from white, wispy mares' tails to towering, leaden, grey thunderclouds. There is such an amazing variety of clouds that no single system of classification could ever do it justice – yet none has been found to improve the system devised by the English pharmacist Luke Howard in 1803. Howard identified ten distinct categories of cloud, all of which are variations on three basic cloud forms – puffy cumulus clouds, stratus clouds forming in layers, and feathery cirrus clouds. This system proved so simple and effective that it is still used by meteorologists today.

LUKE HOWARD (1772–1864)
A keen amateur meteorologist, Howard devised his system by regularly observing clouds and analyzing their shapes and heights.

FLYING SAUCERS
Lenticular clouds (pp. 54–55), so-called because they look like lenses, always form in the lee of mountains.

TRANSLUCENT CLOUD
Altostratus are high, thin sheets of cloud that can often completely cover the sky, so that the sun looks as if it is seen through misty glass. At a warm front (pp. 32–33), lower, thicker, nimbostratus, rain clouds normally follow.

Cloud spreads out at the top where the air stops rising at the tropopause (pp. 6–7). This is sometimes called the "anvil", because it is shaped like an old blacksmith's anvil

Temperature here -40°C (-40°F)

FLEECY CLOUDS *left*
Altocumulus are puffs and rolls of cloud, visible at medium heights. Unlike the higher, smaller cirrocumulus, they always have dark, shadowed sides.

A GREY BLANKET *left*
Stratus is a vast, dull type of cloud that hangs low over the ground and may give a damp drizzle, but no real rain. Higher up, on hills or even from tall buildings, stratus simply appears as fog.

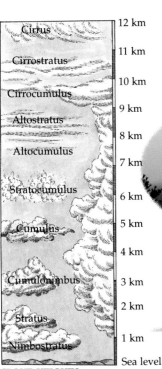

Cirrus	12 km
Cirrostratus	11 km
	10 km
Cirrocumulus	9 km
Altostratus	8 km
Altocumulus	7 km
Stratocumulus	6 km
Cumulus	5 km
	4 km
Cumulonimbus	3 km
	2 km
Stratus	1 km
Nimbostratus	Sea level

CLOUD HEIGHTS
Cirrus-type clouds, including cirrocumulus and cirrostratus, form at the top of the troposphere, where it is coldest. Altostratus and altocumulus are found at medium heights, stratocumulus, stratus, nimbostratus, and cumulus closer to the ground (pp. 6–7). Cumulonimbus may reach up through the whole troposphere.

Temperature here 0°C (32°F)

TRAILING VIRGA
Cumulus clouds sometimes let rain or ice crystals fall into drier, slower-moving layers of air. The streaks that result, known as "virga", evaporate before they reach the ground, and from below look as if they are vanishing into thin air.

MARES' TAILS
Cirrus clouds form high in the sky where the atmosphere is so cold that they are made entirely from ice crystals. Strong winds blow the crystals into wispy "mares' tails".

AN ICY VEIL
Cirrostratus occurs when cirrus spreads into a thin, milky sheet. Here the sun appears very bright and may have one or more coloured rings, or "haloes", around it and, occasionally, brilliant "mock suns" (pp. 58–59).

Mainly ice crystals

Cloud moves from left to right

Strong updraughts carry billows of cloud high into the atmosphere

Mixture of ice crystals and water

HIGH, FLUFFY CLOUDS *right*
Cirrocumulus are tiny, high clumps of shadowless cloud. They consist of ice crystals, like all cirrus clouds, and often form in beautiful, regular waves and ripples, known as a "mackerel sky" – because they look like the mottled scales of the mackerel.

SHOWER CLOUDS *left*
Bigger and darker than cumulus, cumulonimbus usually bring showers of rain – nimbus means "rain" in Latin. Sometimes they grow huge and unleash sudden, gigantic thunderstorms.

A LAYER OF CUMULUS
Stratocumulus often form when the tops of cumulus clouds rise and spread out sideways into broad sheets. Looking down from an aeroplane, they appear as an undulating blanket of rolls and pancakes of cloud, with narrow breaks sometimes showing a glimpse of the ground.

Violent updraughts and downdraughts in the front wall of cloud create hailstones (pp. 36–37)

Mainly water droplets

CAULIFLOWER CLOUDS
Cumulus clouds often mass together and grow upwards with dense, white heads, looking just like cauliflowers. If they keep on growing, they may become rain-bearing cumulonimbus.

Air drawn in here

A rainy day

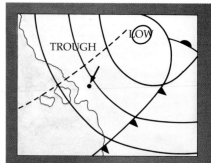

SOMBRE, SLATE-GREY CLOUDS are a sure sign of imminent rain. Clouds like this are dark because they are so deep and full of water that no sunlight penetrates them. The heaviest downpours fall from the deepest, darkest clouds which have all the height needed for raindrops to develop properly. In the tropics, huge cumulonimbus clouds often tower 15 km (9 miles) into the sky, and can unleash a deluge of 0.9 m (3 ft) in an afternoon. The duration and intensity of showers varies greatly. Blankets of lighter, thinner nimbostratus clouds tend to give slower, steadier rain that may last for hours, and even days, on end. Low stratus can envelop you in a persistent drizzle that is little more than a mist.

POURING PETS
The strong updraughts that bring heavy rain have been known to lift creatures as large as frogs and fish up into the air. But no-one claims the old English saying, *Raining cats, dogs, and pitchforks*, is literally true. It may be based on the ancient Chinese spirits for rain and wind, which were sometimes depicted as a cat and a dog.

SOAKING
Meteorologists describe rain as light, if less than 0.5 mm (1/48 in) falls in an hour, and heavy if more than 4 mm (1/6 in) falls. In the mid-latitudes, heavy rain does not usually last for more than an hour or so. Only moderate or light rain persists. Even the worst downpours are rarely heavier than those experienced almost every day in many tropical areas.

Heavy rain can saturate the air beneath the cloud to the extent that further condensation takes place into cloud beneath the main base

CLOUD BURST *right*
The strong updraughts and downdraughts inside a huge, grey cumulonimbus create dramatic and ominously swirling cloud formations – and generally heavy rains. Clouds like this often form along cold fronts (pp. 34–35) and in their wake.

The rough texture of the cloud base indicates just how violent the vertical air currents are within the clouds

OUT ON THE TILES
Exceptionally heavy rain can bring flooding to low-lying districts – especially when the rain comes after a long, dry period. After a drought, the soil can be baked so hard that rain water cannot drain away properly. Instead, it runs off across the surface.

DEEP WATER *right*
Rainfall is usually measured by recording the depth of water that collects in a rain-gauge. A rain-gauge is simply a drum about 50 cm (20 in) tall set on the ground just high enough to avoid splashes. Rain water is caught in the funnel at the top and runs down into a measuring cylinder.

Water runs down funnel and is collected in the cylinder below

lls of cloud develop as falling rain sweeps
der air down towards the ground, forcing
rm air upwards to start off another cloud

Rain falling from the
base of the cloud

This man with his
geese (from a
Japanese
woodcut)
knows that
rain is on the
way, and has
his umbrella
ready

STORM WATERS

Some of the worst floods are
caused, not by rain but by storms
at sea. Huge waves form and the
surging waters swamp coastal
regions (pp. 44–45).

DELUGE

Some of the most torrential rain of all is
brought by the monsoon winds (pp. 38–39).
Monsoon rains bring record rainfalls to places
like Cherrapunji in northeast India which was
once soaked by 4.8 m (16 ft) of rain in 15 days.

Fronts and lows

IN THE MID-LATITUDES OF THE WORLD – between the tropics and the polar regions – much of the year's foulest, most unpleasant weather comes from great, spiralling weather systems which are called depressions or lows. Particularly in winter, "families" of depressions whirl in from the west like giant Catherine wheels, bringing with them cooler weather, cloudy skies, blustery winds, rain, and even snow. A big depression may be hundreds of kilometres wide, but it sweeps quickly across the countryside, usually passing overhead in less than 24 hours, bringing a now well-known sequence of weather.

Warm front

Wisps of cirrus

Veils of cirrostratus

Wind here light and blowing away from the front

Cold polar air

WISPY WARNING
When long streaks of cirrus are seen high in the sky, they often herald a change of weather and the onset of a depression. Cirrus clouds form right at the top of a warm front, so high above the ground that they are composed entirely of ice.

Wind here blowing strong almost parallel to the front

A warm front

The first feature of a depression to arrive is usually a warm front. Here, warm, moist air from the tropics slides up over a wedge of cold, polar air, gradually condensing and forming clouds right up the wedge. The whole front advances steadily forward across the countryside, with the warm air moving over the cold air. At the leading edge of the front, high in the sky, wispy cirrus clouds form, and streaks of high-altitude cirrus are usually the first signs of an approaching depression. Soon after, a milky veil of cirrostratus clouds can be seen. Within a few hours, the air pressure has started to drop, and the wind is blowing harder. As the base of the front nears, the clouds thicken, first with altostratus, then great, grey nimbostratus. The sky grows dark and threatening, and rain – or even snow – starts to fall. The rain lasts several hours before finally clearing up to give a short break before the cold front arrives.

ntinued on next page

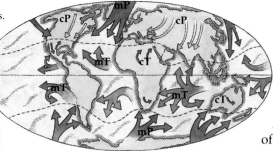

Tropical continental (cT) Polar continental (cP)
Tropical maritime (mT) Polar maritime (mP)

Masses of air

There is a close link between the direction of the wind and the weather. In the mid-latitudes, for instance, westerly winds generally bring rain and storms. Wind and weather are linked by air masses, which are vast chunks of the atmosphere almost uniformly wet or dry, cold or warm throughout. Dry, cold air masses form over continents near the poles, for instance, while warm, moist ones form over tropical oceans. All the world can be divided into areas dominated by particular air masses, each giving its own kind of weather, whether it is biting cold, or warm and wet. To a large extent the weather depends on which air mass is overhead at the time. Far inland, a single air mass can stay in place for long periods at a time, bringing stable weather. In coastal areas, a shift in wind direction often brings in the influence of a different air mass and a change in the weather. The most changeable, stormy weather tends to occur along fronts, where two air masses meet.

CH TO ITS OWN

ch part of the world has its own particular air mass.
e nature of each air mass, and the kind of
eather it brings, depends on whether it forms
er land or sea, near the cold poles or in the
rm tropics. Warm, wet, tropical ocean air
ngs warm, humid weather, while cold, wet,
lar ocean air can bring snow. North America's
st coast, near the meeting point of several air
sses, experiences changeable weather.

ILED WARNING

hen the sun is faintly visible through a thin veil
altostratus, it is time to begin seeking shelter,
r the rain is not far away.

FIRST RAIN
As the front approaches, the sky darkens and the first drops of rain may begin to fall – even before the thickest nimbostratus clouds arrive.

Cold air descending locally at the front

Thickening altostratus

Warm tropical air riding up over the cold air

Dark, rain-bearing nimbostratus

Rain falls in the cold sector beneath the front

Aneroid barometer dial indicating changeable, possibly stormy weather

FALLING DIAL

Long before meteorologists understood the nature of depressions, sailors used barometers to warn them of an imminent storm. They knew that a rapid drop in air pressure was a sure sign of bad weather to come, even if they did not know exactly why. The barometer is still the most reliable way for amateur meteorologists to predict storms.

CHANGE Fair
Much Rain Rain Set Fair
STORMY VERY DRY
29 30 31
28 25
27 26
SOLOMONS & Co CALCUTTA

33

A cold front

After the warm front has passed, the weather becomes milder, and the air pressure drops more slowly. The sky brightens a little as thick nimbostratus give way to stratocumulus. Before long, the clouds may clear away altogether. But the lull is short-lived. Thickening cumulus clouds warn of the coming cold front, where cold polar air cuts in sharply beneath the warm, moist tropical air. The cold front slopes much more steeply than the warm front, and strong updraughts can stir up violent storms. Huge cumulonimbus may build up all along the front, bringing heavy rain and even thunderstorms as it passes over. But though the storms can be intense, the worst is usually over within an hour or so. As the front moves away, the air becomes colder and soon the clouds blow away, leaving just a few fair-weather cumulus scudding across the sky.

High-level winds blow the icy tops of the clouds out in a sharp wedge

Huge cumulonimbus clouds

Advancing cold front

Rapidly rising warm air

BREWING STORM
There is no mistaking the towering grey cumulonimbus clouds that build up along a cold front. Although the foreground here is calm, the horizon is dark with rain as the front approaches.

Winds along the front are often strong and gusty

Heavy rain falls in various places all along the cold front

ON THE LINE
Cold fronts tend to bring sudden, violent gusts of wind and rain known as squalls. Storms along the front often advance in a clear edge called a squall line.

Continued from previous page

*Strong updraughts
carry moisture up so
far that it turns to ice*

SUNSET CALM
As the front moves away
to the east, the skies clear,
leaving just a few puffy
cumulus clouds towards
the setting sun. High
above, the strong upper
atmosphere winds driving
the depression create
dramatic streaks of icy
clouds across the sky.

*The air grows colder
and the pressure rises
behind the front*

*Cold polar air
sharply undercuts
the warm tropical air*

*Showers may still fall
from bigger cumulus
clouds even after the
front has passed*

These diagrams show the sequence in
the northern hemisphere; for the south,
hold a mirror above each picture.

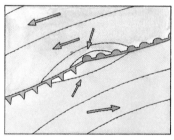

1. Depressions start with a bulge in
the polar front, where cold polar air
and warm tropical air meet.

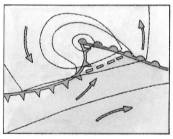

2. Spun by the Coriolis Effect
(pp. 42–43), the two air masses rotate
round a deepening low pressure area.

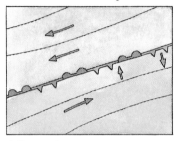

3. The kink in the front develops two
arms – the warm front and the cold
front – and moves slowly eastwards.

The life of
a depression

Many depressions begin their lives over the
sea. Here, warm, moist, tropical air masses and
cold, dry, polar air masses collide along an imaginary line
called the "polar front". A depression starts when the tropical air
bulges polewards into the polar air. As the warm tropical air rises over
the cold polar air, it creates an area of low pressure at the crest of the bulge. The
polar air rushes in behind to replace the rising warm air. Soon winds begin to spiral
around the low pressure centre as cold chases warm. The depression deepens, and the
polar front starts to develop a definite kink. Along one edge, the warm air continues to ride
slowly forward over the cold air in a gradual slope (the warm front). Along the other, the
cold air thrusts sharply under the warm air from behind (the cold front). The depression
deepens further and is drawn slowly eastwards by strong winds in the upper atmosphere.

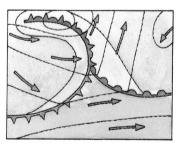

4. Eventually the cold front catches
up with the warm front, lifting it
off the ground to create an
"occluded" front.

Thunder and lightning

WHEN A BLACK, LOWERING CUMULONIMBUS CLOUD UNLEASHES its deluge of thunder, lightning, wind, and rain, the effect can be truly awe-inspiring. Big thunderclouds tower 16 km (10 miles) or more in the air – occasionally through the tropopause into the stratosphere (pp. 6–7) – and churn within them enough energy to light a small town for a year. Building up a cloud of such phenomenal depth and power demands tremendously vigorous updraughts – the kind that often occur along cold fronts or above areas of ground heated especially strongly by hot sunshine. This is why, in the tropics, massive thunderstorms often break in the afternoon, after a morning's sun has stirred up the air. Inland, in the temperate zone, a long spell of hot weather often ends in a tumult of thunder and lightning.

THUNDERSTRUCK
The heavy hammer wielded by Thor, the Norse god of thunder, represented the "thunderbolt" once thought to fall from the clouds.

IT'S ELECTRIC!
In 1752, Benjamin Franklin had a lucky escape when proving that lightning was electricity. He flew a silk kite in a thunderstorm and saw sparks jumping from a key on the string to his hand.

STORM GOD
To ward off violent storms and tropical downpours, Yoruba priests in south-western Nigeria held ceremonies around images of the thunder-and-lightning god Sango.

STRIKE!
Lightning tends to strike tall objects, such as isolated trees – which is why it is dangerous to shelter under one in a storm.

LIGHTNING GENERATOR
Thunderclouds are heaving masses of air, water, and ice. Inside, ice crystals are swept up and down by the violent air currents and grow into hailstones, as water freezes around them in layers like the skins of an onion. Ice crystals and water droplets are torn apart and then smashed together with such ferocity that they become charged with static electricity. Light, positively-charged pieces of ice and water tend to pile up towards the top of the cloud, and heavier, negatively-charged pieces accumulate at the base. The ground below is also positively-charged. The difference in electrical charges eventually becomes so great that they are neutralized by lightning flashing within the cloud (sheet lightning), or between the cloud and the ground (fork lightning).

HAVING A BALL

Throughout history, many people have reported seeing a strange phenomenon called ball lightning. In 1773, just after a clap of thunder, two clergy-men saw a tiny, bright ball, no bigger than a football, glow in the fireplace, then burst with a bang. No-one can explain these rare sightings.

HAIL AND HEARTY
A section of the largest hailstone ever
found, which weighed 768 g (1.7 lb) and
fell in Coffeyville, Kansas, USA in 1970.
Special illumination shows its internal
structure of alternating layers of clear
and opaque ice.

*Cumulonimbus
clouds still
growing upward*

STORM SHOOTING
Hail can devastate crops.
Around 1900, many people
shot debris into the
clouds to stop the
hail forming.
These anti-hail
guns injured
people on the
ground, but
the hail was
just as heavy.

*As a lightning bolt flashes
through the air, the air around
becomes five times as hot as
the surface of the sun. The air
expands at supersonic speed,
making the mighty crash
called thunder*

*A split second after the
leader stroke, a massive
surge of lightning – the
"return stroke" – shoots up
the path it created*

*Lightning always takes
the easiest path from
cloud to ground*

*Lightning bolts begin
when a small "leader
stroke" zig-zags to the
ground, ionizing
(charging) the air and
completing a circuit*

Monsoon

TROPICAL STORM
The monsoon can lash tropical coasts with intense rain, wind, thunder, and lightning.

For six months of the year, most of India is parched and dry. But, every May, the monsoon comes. A moist wind starts to blow in from the Indian Ocean and the skies over the southwest coast grow dark with clouds. For six months, showers of torrential rain sweep north over the country, right up to the foothills of the Himalayas – until, in October, the southwest wind dies down and the rains slacken. By the end of the year, the land is dry once more. The monsoon is especially marked in India, but similar rainy seasons occur in many other places in the tropics, including northeast Australia, East Africa, and the southern United States.

The monsoon brings some of the world's most torrential rains

Band of rain moving rapidly across open grassland

DRAGON'S BREATH
The monsoon rains are vital for agriculture in most of Asia. To the Chinese their importance was symbolized by the dragon, a creature of the heavens and of the rivers – at times violent, but also the bringer of the precious gift of water.

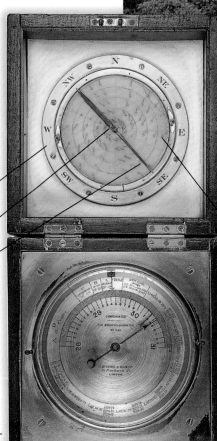

Typhoon barometer

Wind disc for tracking the path of the typhoon

Heavy needle lines up with the normal path of storms in the region

Thin needle indicates safe course away from the storm

Arrows on the disc for the direction of the wind over the ship. The disc is turned until a arrow crosses the heavy needle in the right direction

TYPHOON TRACKER
Ships at sea around many monsoon regions often fall foul of ferocious, fast-moving tropical cyclones. To help them track the path of the storm and steer a safe course many ships used to carry an instrument like this, called a "baryocyclometer". Now m rely on broadcast warnings.

AFTER THE DELUGE
Monsoon rain can be so intense that floods are frequent. In India and Bangladesh, the delta of the river Ganges is in particular danger of being flooded, especially if a storm surge occurs at the same time (pp. 44–45).

High cumulonimbus clouds

Mountains force the monsoon upward causing even more rain: Cherrapunji in the Assam mountains is one of the wettest places in the world

Large cumulonimbus clouds pile up against high ground as the monsoon blows inland

Some areas may stay dry and parched even while neighbouring areas are being drenched

⌐HE MONSOON COMES

⌐onsoons are like giant sea breezes (pp. 56–57). The rains begin when ⌐mmer sun heats up tropical continents far faster than the oceans around. ⌐arm air rising over land draws in cool, moist air from the sea, and rain-⌐aring winds gradually push farther inland. A monsoon's onset is hard to ⌐edict, and sometimes it fails to bring any rain to the hot, drought-stricken ⌐nds that year. Then crops fail, with a great danger of famine. Asian mon-⌐ons may be triggered off when westerly jet streams in the upper air swing ⌐rth over the Himalayas.

⌐ONSOON REGION

⌐onsoons affect
⌐ge areas of the
⌐pics and the
⌐b-tropics
⌐m northeast
⌐stralia to the
⌐ribbean. Asian
⌐onsoons are the most
⌐arked, because Asia is so vast.

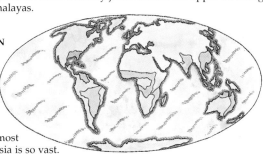

SOUTHWEST MONSOON
The hot, dry lands of Asia draw warm air, laden with moisture, in from the Indian Ocean during the early summer.

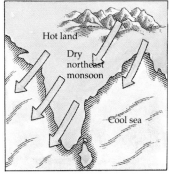

NORTHEAST MONSOON
The cold, dry winter air spreads out from central Asia, bringing chilly, dusty conditions to the lands around.

A snowy day

IN THE DEPTHS OF WINTER, driving snow and blizzards may fall from the same grey clouds and fronts that in summer brought welcome showers. Outside the tropics, most rain starts off as snow, melting as it drops into warmer air. When snow falls, the air is just cold enough to let the flakes flutter to the ground before they melt. Sometimes, snow can be falling on the mountaintop while down in the valley it is raining. People often say the weather is "too cold for snow", and there is some truth in this, since very cold air may not hold enough moisture for any kind of precipitation (pp. 22-23). In fact, more snow falls in a year in southern Canada and the northern USA than at the North Pole. The heaviest snowfalls occur when the air temperature is hovering around freezing – which is why snow can be hard to forecast, because a rise in temperature of just a few degrees above freezing may bring rain instead.

ST. BERNARDS TO THE RESCUE
Freshly fallen snow contains so much air that people can survive for a long time beneath it.

Under very cold conditions snow remains loose and powdery, and is often whipped up by the wind

Fresh snow can contain as much as 90-95 per cent air, and acts as an insulator, protecting the ground from much colder temperatures above the surface

RIVERS OF ICE AND AIR
Snow accumulates on high ground where temperatures are low. It becomes compacted into ice, which slowly flows down valleys as glaciers. The air above large ice-caps becomes very cold and heavy, and follows the same paths, bringing icy winds to the lowlands beneath.

A COLD BLANKET
Once snow has covered the ground, it is often slow to melt, because it reflects away most of the sunlight. If the surface melts partially and then refreezes, the snow-cover will last even longer. Only the arrival of a warm air-mass is really effective in melting the snow.

SNOWFLAKES
Snowflakes occur in an infinite variety of shapes, and no-one has ever found two the same. All natural snowflakes are six-sided, and consist of ice crystals which are flat plates, although rarer forms like needles and columns are sometimes found.

THE SNOWFLAKE MAN
W. A. Bentley was an American farmer who spent every possible moment out in the cold, photographing snowflakes through a microscope. Over 40 years he obtained many thousands of photographs.

990 mb   Cloudy   Strong winds

"Tablecloth" of stratus cloud caused by gentle airflow over the mountains

On average, 30.5 cm (12 in) of snow is equal to 2.54 cm (1 in) of rain

Harder surface crust caused by melting and refreezing

Eddies in the wind always cause more snow to fall in one place than in another, leading to drifts, which tend to grow larger and larger.

AVALANCHE

The greatest danger of avalanches comes when fresh, loose snow has fallen onto a harder, icy layer. The slightest disturbance can start a slide, which crashes down into the valley, burying anything and anyone in its path. The blast of air in front of it is often strong enough to demolish buildings.

BLIZZARD

In blizzard conditions, snowfall is accompanied by strong winds, and it may become impossible to see anything, causing chaos for transport and communications in both cities and the countryside. The wind piles up huge drifts of snow against any obstacles, and may completely cover cars and trains, trapping the passengers inside.

Wind

THE WORLD'S ATMOSPHERE is forever on the move. Wind is air in motion. Sometimes air moves slowly, giving a gentle breeze. At other times it moves rapidly, creating gales and hurricanes (pp. 44–45). Gentle or fierce, wind always starts in the same way. As the sun moves through the sky, it heats up some parts of the sea and land more than others. The air above these hot spots is warmed, becomes lighter than the surrounding air, and begins to rise. Elsewhere, cool air sinks, because it is heavier. Winds blow because air squeezed out by sinking, cold air is sucked in under rising, warm air. Winds will blow wherever there is a difference in air temperature and pressure, always flowing from high to low pressure. Some winds blow in one place, and have a local name – France's Mistral and North America's Chinook. Others are part of a huge circulation pattern that sends winds over the entire globe.

TOWER OF THE WINDS
In the 1st century B.C., the Greek astronomer Andronicus built a Horologium, or Tower Winds. The tower was octagonal (eight-sided) and on each face was carved one of the eight wind spirits, one for ea direction the wind blew Boreas (north wind) an Notos (south wind) we the main winds.

High up, strong jet streams circle the globe

Polar front

Polar winds

Warm tropical air flowing to poles

Westerlies Easterly trade winds

WORLD WINDS
The world's winds are part of a global system of air circulation that moves warm air from the equator to the poles and cold air the opposite way, keeping temperatures around the world in balance. At the poles, cold air sinks and moves towards the equator. At the equator, warm air rises and moves towards the poles high in the atmosphere. As it moves away from the equator it cools and sinks towards the surface over the sub-tropics. Here some continues to flow polewards, and some flows back towards the equator. Because the Earth is spinning, winds bend to the right north of the equator and to the left in the south. This is called the Coriolis Effect, and bends every wind on Earth. So the winds blowing towards the equator from the subtropics (trade winds) become northeasterlies north of the equator and southeasterlies to the south. Winds blowing polewards from the sub-tropics in the mid-latitudes become westerlies.

Head points into the wind, indicating the direction the wind is blowing from

VANE WARNING
Perhaps the oldest of all meteorological instruments, weather vanes swing around in the wind to show where it is blowing from. In Christian countries, vanes are often in the form of weather cocks like this. Weather cocks first adorned church roofs in the ninth century A.D., and were intended a a perpetual reminder of the cock that crow when St. Peter denied Christ three times. Now they are seen in all kinds of places, an the religious symbolism is largely forgotten

CATCHING THE WIND
Long, thin flags like this, called pennants, or bourgues, were often flown on sailing ships to show which way the wind was blowing. They were often decorative a well as functional, and in the 17th century many big ships were festooned with them. In the Middle Ages, similar colourful pennants would flutter over battlefields. They showed archers the wind direction so that they could take this into account when aiming their bows.

Cross indicating north, east, south, and west

Wind strength scale

Swinging ball

40
30
20
18
16
15
14
13
12
11
10
9
8
7
6
5 4
3
2
0 1

METRES PER SECOND

WIND INSTRUMENT

Swinging-arm anemometers, or wind gauges, may be the earliest devices for measuring wind strength. The Italian, Leon Alberti, wrote about one around 1450. The ball, or pressure plate, swings in the wind along the curved scale. The stronger the wind, the higher the ball swings.

Fin to keep the meter facing into the wind

WIND SCALE

In 1805, the British Admiral Sir Francis Beaufort devised a scale for measuring winds at sea by observing their effects on sailing ships and waves. Beaufort's scale was later adapted for use on land and is still used today by many weather stations. Wind strengths are divided into 12 forces: Force 1 (light air); Force 2 (light breeze); Force 3 (gentle breeze); Force 4 (moderate breeze); Force 5 (fresh breeze); Force 6 (strong breeze); Force 7 (near gale); Force 8 (gale); Force 9 (strong gale); Force 10 (storm); Force 11 (violent storm); Force 12 (hurricane).

Force 6 is a strong breeze, giving some large waves and white horses at sea

Force 10 is a storm, causing high waves with long overhanging crests

Cups spin round at high speed – just how fast depends on the strength of the wind

WIND MILL

Now most weather stations measure wind speed using spinning cup anemometers, invented in 1846. As the cups rotate, the spindle triggers an electrical contact, so that the number of rotations in a given time is recorded. This 19th-century instrument is an anemograph, and the speed is continuously recorded as a cylindrical chart driven by clockwork.

Complete calm is Force 0 on the Beaufort Scale

The average wind speed is recorded on graph paper as this cylinder rotates

CHINESE FLIERS

The ancient Chinese were flying kites in the wind as long ago as 500 B.C. Some were made in the shape of dragons to frighten enemies. Others were made large enough to carry observers aloft, and some were made in the shape of socks to indicate the strength and direction of the wind, just like modern windsocks at airports and aerodromes. Today, kites are mainly flown as toys.

Rotors turn wind vane into the wind

Wind vane to show wind direction

AIR POWER

Windmills usually face into the prevailing wind – that is, in the direction of the wind that blows most often.

Tropical storms

Hurricane force winds often damage buildings

KNOWN AS TYPHOONS IN THE PACIFIC, and tropical cyclones by meteorologists, hurricanes claim more lives each year than any other storms. When a full-blown hurricane strikes, trees are ripped up and buildings flattened by raging winds, gusting up to 360 kph (220 mph). Vast areas are swamped by torrential rain, and coastal regions can be completely overwhelmed by the "storm surge". This is a mound of water some 8 m (25 ft) high, sucked up by the storm's "eye" – the ring of low pressure at the storm's centre – and topped by giant waves whipped up by the winds. Hurricanes begin as small thunderstorms over warm, tropical oceans. If the water is warm enough (over 24°C or 75°F), several storms may cluster together and whirl around as one, encouraged by strong winds high in the atmosphere. Soon they drift westwards across the ocean, drawing in warm, moist air and spinning in ever tighter circles. At first the centre of the storm may be over 300 km (200 miles) across, and the winds barely gale force. As it moves west, it gains energy from the warm air it sucks in. By the time the storm reaches the far side of the ocean, the eye has shrunk to 50 km (30 miles) across, pressure there has dropped dramatically, and winds howl around it at hurricane force.

ANATOMY OF A HURRICANE
The air in the eye of the hurricane is at low pressure, and is calm. As the eye passes over, the winds may drop altogether, and a small circle of clear sky may be visible overhead for a while. The lull is short-lived, however, as torrential rains fall around the eye, and raging winds, drawn in from hot air that spirals up the wall of the eye, circulate at speeds of 50 kph (30 mph). The rain and wind are at their worst right next to the eye of the storm, but spiralling bands of rain and wind can occur up to 400 km (240 miles) away. It can be 18 hours or more before the storm has passed over completely.

MIXED BLESSING
The vegetation and agriculture on many tropical islands depend on the torrential rains brought by hurricanes. But the terrible winds can also ravage crops, and only a few – like bananas – recover quickly.

The strongest winds, with gusts up to 360 kph (220 mph), are found beneath the eye wall, immediately outside the eye.

HURRICANE WATCH
Thanks to satellite images, meteorologists can detect hurricanes when they are far from land, and track them as they approach. Special aircraft repeatedly fly through the storm to obtain accurate measurements that help predict its violence and likely path. Since 1954, names have been given to all tropical storms to prevent confusion when issuing forecasts and evacuation warnings.

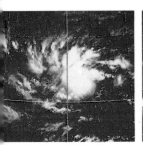

Day 1: thunderstorms develop over the sea.

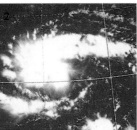

Day 2: storms group to form a swirl of cloud.

Day 4: winds grow, distinct centre forms in cloud swirl.

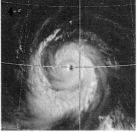

Day 7: eye forms, typhoon is at its most dangerous.

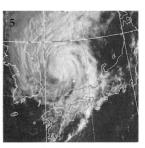

Day 11: eye passes over land, typhoon starts to decay.

ice forms at the very top of the clouds

A vast, circular shield of clouds is caused by air billowing from the top of the storm and spreading out

Eye wall

Spiral rain bands

Warm, moist air spirals up around the eye inside the hurricane

Hurricanes are enormous. Some may be as much as 800 km (480 miles) across

The heat contained by the warm sea provides the energy needed to drive the whole storm

Calm eye of hurricane, where winds may be no more than 25 kph (15 mph)

Air descends in the eye, leaving it clear of cloud

Winds well above 160 kph (100 mph) occur over a large area beneath the storm

PACIFIC HURRICANE
The sequence above shows satellite images of a typhoon over the Pacific Ocean. It begins when water evaporates over vast areas of the ocean in the hot, tropical sun to produce huge, cumulonimbus clouds and bands of thunderstorms (1). Gradually, a swirl of clouds develops, and the growing storm looks like a vigorous, ordinary depression (pp. 32–33) (2). The winds become even stronger, and rotate around a single centre (3). Eventually an eye develops, just inside the ring of the most destructive and violent winds (4). When such a storm passes over land – in this case, Japan – or over cold seas, it loses its source of energy, and the winds drop rapidly (5).

ALBANY HURRICANE
Hurricanes were far more dangerous when their approach was unexpected. In 1940, the fringes of a hurricane struck Albany in Georgia, USA, without adequate warning, wrecking large numbers of buildings, including big hotels, and killing several people. Two years before, 600 people were killed in New England by a sudden, fast-moving storm.

Whirling winds

TORNADOES GO BY MANY NAMES – twisters, whirlwinds, and more. Wherever they strike, these whirling spirals of wind leave a trail of unbelievable destruction. They roar past in just a few minutes, tossing people, cars, and strong buildings high into the air, then smashing them to the ground. Meteorological instruments rarely survive to tell what conditions are really like in a tornado. Winds probably race around the outside at over 400 kph (240 mph), while pressure at the centre plunges several hundred millibars lower than outside. This creates a kind of funnel, or vortex, that acts like a giant vacuum clean sucking things into the air, tearing the tops off trees, and blowing out windows. Tornadoes har down like an elephant's trunk from giant thunderclouds, and may strik wherever thunderstorms occur.

MILD SPIN
Tornadoes are especially violent in the central USA, but they can occur anywhe there are thunderstorms, as this engravin of an English whirlwind shows.

Supercell cloud

1 SWIRLING COLUMN
Tornadoes start deep within vast thunderclouds, where a column of strongly rising warm air is set spinning by high winds streaming through the cloud's top. As air is sucked into this swirling column, or mesocyclone, it spins very fast, stretching thousands of metres up and down through the cloud, with a corkscrewing funnel descending from the cloud's base – the tornado.

CROP CIRCLES
For centuries, it has been a mystery why perfect circles of flattened crops appear at random in the summer. A few people believe that it may be whirling winds which cause them.

Cloud b

2 WHIRLING DERVISH
Soon the funnel touches down, and the tremendous updraught in its centre swirls dust, debris, cars, and people high into the sky. Chunks of wood and other objects become deadly missiles as they are hurled through the air by the ferocious winds. A tornado deals destruction ver selectively – reducing houses in its path to matchwood and rubble, yet leaving those just a few metres outside its path completely untouched. Sometimes a tornado will whirl things high into the air, then set them gently down, unharmed, hundreds of metres away.

WATERSPOUT

When a tornado occurs over the sea, it becomes a waterspout. These often last longer than tornadoes, but tend to be gentler, with wind speeds less than 80 kph (50 mph). This may be because water is heavier than air, and the strong temperature contrasts needed to create violent updraughts are less marked over water than land.

DUSTY MENACE
Unlike tornadoes and waterspouts which spin down from clouds, "dust devils" are formed in the desert by columns of hot air whirling up from the ground. Far weaker than tornadoes, they can still cause damage. Whirling devils also occur over snow and water, although these can start as violent eddies whipping up from the surface.

FLYING ROOFS *left and above*
In the strong winds of tornadoes, the roofs of houses generate lift, just like the wings of a plane. When the roof is whisked away, the rest of the house disintegrates. Stronger roofs, more firmly anchored to the buildings beneath, would prevent a great deal of damage.

Funnel touching down in a whirling spray of dust and debris

3 SPINNING VORTEX
For a moment, the funnel has lifted away from the ground, and the houses beneath are safe. But at any instant it may touch down again. This is a large tornado, and within it there is not just one spinning vortex but several, each revolving around the rim of the main one.

Fogs and mists

BEACON IN THE DARK
Thick, persistent fog can form over such sea areas as southwestern Britain, the Banks off Newfoundland, and Tierra del Fuego at the tip of South America. In really dense fog, the lights of lighthouses warning ships of hazards, may be lost in the dark, and sailors must rely on sirens and foghorns.

Wͤᴇɴ ᴛʜᴇ ᴡɪɴᴅ is light, skies are clear, and the air is damp, moisture in the air can often condense near the ground to form mist or fog, especially at dawn or dusk. In some places, dawn often breaks with thick mist hanging over the landscape like a pale, grey veil – only dispersing as the sun begins to warm the air and stir up stronger winds. Sometimes fog forms because the ground cools down enough to bring the air to its dew point (pp. 22–23), and the fog spreads slowly upwards. This is called radiation fog, and often occurs on clear, fairly calm nights in areas where there is plenty of moisture, such as river valleys, lakes, and harbours. Fog can also form by advection, where a warm, moist wind blows over a cooler surface.

Over the sea, temperature does not always fall far enough to form fog

CALIFORNIA FOG
In San Francisco, USA, the distinctive towers of the Golden Gate Bridge often rise above the thick mist that rolls in from the Pacific. This fog is an advection fog, and forms because warm, moist air from the south blows over cool ocean currents flowing down from the Arctic. As it moves inland, the fog evaporates quickly over the warm surface of the land, and usually thins out as it is blown in towards San Francisco. On the coast, advection fogs may take time to disperse – unlike radiation fogs – because they will break up only when there is a change in the conditions that caused them.

SMOG MASK
Urban areas are particularly prone to thick fogs, not only because they are often situated in low-lying areas close to water, but also fog forms much more readily when there are plenty of condensation nuclei (pp. 22–23) in the air. In some cities, the huge quantities of airborne particles released by car exhausts, fires, and industry make some cyclists wear masks. They also form very good condensation nuclei for fog.

PEA-SOUPER
Heavy industry and millions of coal fires once made London so dirty that the city was famous for its fogs "as thick as pea-soup", when visibility would drop to 15 m (50 ft) or less. During the 1950s, government decisions to clean up the air have reduced the number of fogs dramatically, and such pea-soupers are now a thing of the past.

Light winds bring in new air to sustain mist

1024 mb Sunny Light wind

Fog is actually tiny droplets of water condensed from the air

Fog spreads slowly upwards from the surface of the water

TWO FOGS
Some coastal fog is a mixture of both radiation and advection fog. On a clear, warm day, a sea breeze may start (pp. 56–57), bringing relatively cool, moist air across the land. At night, most of this drifts back to sea as it is replaced by the drier land air. Some sea air may linger and cool further until it condenses to form fog.

UPSIDE DOWN
Fog forms just above the ground, or water, and spreads slowly upwards, but only so far, because the calm, clear conditions that encourage it to form may also cause a reversal in the normal change in temperature in the atmosphere. The air actually gets warmer around 500 m (1640 ft) above the ground. This is called a temperature inversion, and the base of the inversion marks the ceiling of the fog. Inversions like this are common in places like San Diego (right) in California, USA, and the Sydney basin in Australia.

A day of weather

THE WEATHER CAN CHANGE dramatically during the course of a single day. Sometimes these daily changes can be more striking than any long-term variations. In many tropical regions, the same marked changes in the weather occur regularly day after day, where fine, sunny mornings are almost always followed by a massive build-up of thunderclouds as the sun stirs up strong updraughts. Usually this is followed by a brief deluge in the afternoon and a clear dusk. A similar sequence often occurs in mid-latitudes if the weather is warm and stable. In these areas regular daily changes are often overpowered by the passage of a depression, which can swing the weather from warm sunshine to icy rain in a few hours.

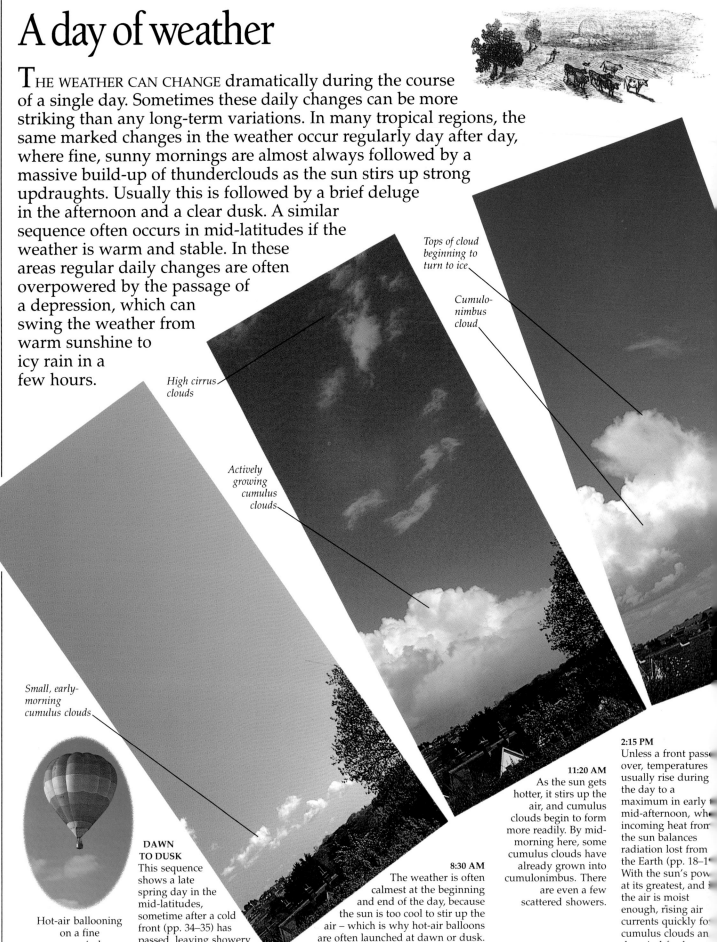

Tops of cloud beginning to turn to ice

Cumulo-nimbus cloud

High cirrus clouds

Actively growing cumulus clouds

Small, early-morning cumulus clouds

Hot-air ballooning on a fine summer's day

DAWN TO DUSK
This sequence shows a late spring day in the mid-latitudes, sometime after a cold front (pp. 34–35) has passed, leaving showery weather in its wake.

8:30 AM
The weather is often calmest at the beginning and end of the day, because the sun is too cool to stir up the air – which is why hot-air balloons are often launched at dawn or dusk.

11:20 AM
As the sun gets hotter, it stirs up the air, and cumulus clouds begin to form more readily. By mid-morning here, some cumulus clouds have already grown into cumulonimbus. There are even a few scattered showers.

2:15 PM
Unless a front passes over, temperatures usually rise during the day to a maximum in early mid-afternoon, when incoming heat from the sun balances radiation lost from the Earth (pp. 18–1 With the sun's pow at its greatest, and the air is moist enough, rising air currents quickly for cumulus clouds an the wind freshens.

*y head of cloud
*pread out by high
vel winds

*Sky thick
with cloud*

*Rain
heavy in
places*

*Sky
starting
to lighten
behind
cloud*

*Sky
starting
to lighten
behind
cloud*

3:00 PM
By mid-afternoon,
clouds can build up to such an
extent that thunderstorms occur. Here,
clusters of clouds have joined together to
make even larger storms, with thunder
and lightning, very heavy rain, and hail
nearby, even if not overhead.

Rain

3:45 PM
The sky is still darkened by a
gigantic, grey cumulonimbus cloud, its
top hidden by the widespread lower
clouds around the edge of the storm,
which is now upon us. Gusts of wind
give warning of the downdraughts and
torrential rain to come.

5:15 PM
The heavy clouds are
beginning to lift and
move away, although
rain is still falling.
Sunlight strikes
through beneath the
edge of the cloud,
illuminating the
raindrops and creating
a rainbow. The worst
of the storm is over.

*Extra, pinkish-
violet bows inside
the primary bow*

ASTLES IN THE AIR
the right conditions, a layer of warm air may
*rm over a cold sea. On the Italian island of
*ily, this can produce a mirage about mid-
*orning called "Fata Morgana". Distorted
*ages of distant objects appear, looking like
*stles or tall buildings. They are created when
*e warm air bends light rays from images of
*jects normally invisible beyond the horizon.

7:00 PM
By sunset, the wind has dropped and
the band of thunderstorms and
showers has moved away,
leaving only a few
scattered cumulus. In
contrast to the clear sky
of the morning,
increasing middle-level
clouds show that a weak
trough of low pressure
is approaching from
the west.

Cirrostratus

Altostratus

Cumulus

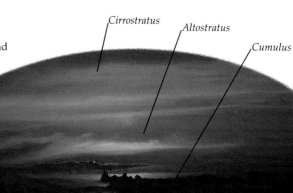

Mountain weather

High up in the atmosphere, pressure drops, winds are ferocious, and the air is bitterly cold. On mountain tops, such as Mount Everest's summit, the air pressure can be as low as 300 mb, winds howl through its crags at up to 320 kph (192 mph), and the temperature often drops to -70°C (-94°F). Even on lower mountains, winds tend to be much stronger than down on the plains. Above a certain height – known as the snowline – many mountains are permanently coated in snow and ice. Because mountains jut so far into the atmosphere, they interfere with wind and cloud patterns, forcing air to move up or down as it passes over their peaks. Air rising up the windward side of a mountain means that lower summits are often shrouded in mist and rain.

Barometer used for measuring air pressure

HIGH READINGS
Many weather stations are sited on mountain tops to record conditions high up in the atmosphere, but they are bleak places. On the summit of Mount Washington in New Hampshire, USA, winds are frequently over 160 kph (96 mph), temperatures are often below -30°C (-22°F), and dense fog is common.

PRESSURE AT THE TOP
In 1648, a French scientist Blaise Pascal proved Torricelli's view (pp. 10–11) that the atmosphere had its own weight, or pressure. If Torricelli was right, Pascal reasoned, the air pressure would be lower at the top of the mountain, because there was less air weighing down on it from above. When he took a barometer up a mountain, the mercury level showing air pressure dropped as expected.

CLOUDS AND SNOW
In many mountain ranges, the highest peaks may project above the tops of the clouds, basking in bright sunshine while clouds fill the valley below. Nothing but a few icy wisps may climb to the summits, and the air is dry and clear. Yet, though sunny, the peaks are usually icy cold, and any heat from the sun is reflected straight back into the atmosphere by the snow. Near the equator, only the very highest peaks – above 5,000 m (16,400 ft) or so – are perpetually covered in snow, as it is too cold here for rain. Towards the poles, however, the snow line gets progressively lower.

Peaks stand clear of the clouds

Wisps of icy cloud

Perpetual snow cover

At night, cold air may drain into the valleys, making them very cold

WET PEAKS
Even when it is not cold, the tops of mountains tend to be wet and misty especially if they poke up into a moist air stream. Pacific island mountains, like these in Tahiti, are among the dampest places in the world. Hawaii's Mount Wai-'ale-'ale is wreathed in moist clouds for 354 days a year, and is soaked annually by more than 11,600 mm (457 in) of rain.

Barometer
very low

A little
cloud
cover

Winds of
165 kph
(99 mph)
or more

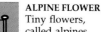

ALPINE FLOWER

Tiny flowers,
called alpines,
have been
very successful
in adapting to
the sunny, cold
weather of
mountains such as
the Alps in
Europe, where
they grow
plentifully in spring.

*North-facing slopes are always in
deep shadow, and bitterly cold –
so cold that ice breaks up the rocks
making them steep and craggy*

*Air pushed up the
mountain slopes often
fills valleys with clouds*

HIGH SIERRA

High up in the mountains, there is often a strong
wind to increase the effect of the chill in the air,
even on the sunniest days. Mountain tops are
nearly always windier than open, low country.
This is partly because wind strength everywhere
increases with height. Winds can be very much
stronger at 1000 m (3280 ft), than at sea level.
Also winds rush over, rather than around, the
tops of mountains, and gain speed as they do so.

*Air warms and dries
as it descends in the lee
of the mountain range*

Leeward side

*Rising air cools
and condenses
into clouds*

*Rain on the
summits*

*oist air
rced
wards by
ountain range*

Windward side

AIR LIFT

When a moist air stream meets a mountain range, it is
forced upwards towards the summit. As it rises, it cools and
may condense into clouds around the summit of the mountains.
Higher-level clouds can then act as "feeder" clouds, letting a little rain fall onto
the summit clouds below. Soon these are raining heavily. Fronts, too, may be disrupted
by mountains. Warm fronts (pp. 32–33) may be broken up when they run up against a
mountain ridge. Cold fronts (pp. 34–35) may deposit so much rain that they die out quickly on the far
side. All this brings rain to the windward side of mountains, and leaves the leeward side much drier.

Weather on the plains

THE GREAT PLAINS of North America, the Steppes of Russia, the Pampas of South America, the grasslands of Australia – these and other vast, flat plains of the world experience weather that is very different from that in the mountains (pp. 52–53). Far from the sea, or cut off from it by high mountains, plains tend to have hot summers and cold winters, and receive little rain. Fronts (pp. 32–35) are broken up by mountain ranges, or lose their energy long before they reach the heart of the plains. What rain there is falls mostly in the summer when strong sun stirs up heavy showers and thunderstorms. In winter, rainfall is rare, although autumn snowstorms may deposit a covering that lasts until spring. In the shadow of mountain ranges, many plains are so dry that only scrub, or grass, can grow.

WINTER HUNTERS
Millions of buffalo once roamed the vast grasslands of North America and provided rich hunting for the many plains Indian tribes, who were well adapted to the cold winters. They would wear snowshoes when hunting to stop their feet sinking into the snow.

Skies are often clear, giving hot days and cold nights

HOT BLAST
Where plains are in the lee of mountains they are often subject to hot winds, warmed as they descend from mountains. The Chinook of the North American Rockies, and the parching Arabian Simoom, shown in this engraving, are typical.

WAVE–CLOUDS
High mountain ranges often disturb winds blowing across them, and set up a pattern of waves that do not move, but hang in the same place in the upper atmosphere. Bands of stationary cloud may form in the crest of each wave.

EXTREME WEATHER
Far from any source of moisture, skies over the plains are often brilliantly clear and blue. This causes natural extremes in temperatu... between summer and winter, day and night. Winters on the plains a... bitter, with temperatures well below freezing and severe frosts for many weeks. In summer, temperatures drop once the sun goes dow...

PARCHED LAN...
Most of the world's gre... deserts are plains, such... North America's Nevad... Here the moist winds... the Pacific are robbed... moisture by the Sier... Nevada, which... between the desert a... the sea. Winds blowi... down the mountains ... warmed so much by the des... that they leave the plains parch... and dry – an effect called "rainshadow...

1000 mb

Some
cloud
cover

Strong
wind

*Smooth, lens-shaped
"lenticular" wave-clouds
often form in bands in the
lee of mountain ranges,
sometimes building up
like piles of plates*

*With little to slow them down,
winds can be very strong in
plains, blowing predominantly
from the mountains*

*Low rainfall leads
to scrubby, stunted
vegetation*

LOW

HIGH

DUST TO DUST

Far from the sea, plains lands are sensitive
to climate changes. Strengthening westerly
winds in the early 20th century increased
the Rocky Mountains' rainshadow effect on
the prairies. Drought in the 1930s brought
disaster to vast areas, creating a "Dust Bowl"
and forcing many families to leave their
farms.

SIZZLING
SUMMERS

Summer on the plains can be extremely hot. In
Death Valley, California (above), temperatures
reached 56.7°C (134°F) in 1913. In Queensland,
Australia, temperatures soared nearly as high at
53.1°C (127.6°F) in 1889. The highest temperature
ever recorded is 58°C (136.4°F) in Libya in 1922.

Weather by the sea

THE PRESENCE OF SO MUCH WATER GIVES weather by the sea its own particular characteristics. Winds blowing in off the sea are naturally moister than those blowing off the land. So coastal areas tend to be noticeably wetter than inland areas – especially if they face into the prevailing wind (pp. 42–43). They can be cloudier, too. Cumulus clouds (pp. 24–25), for instance, usually form inland only during the day, but on coasts facing the wind, they drift overhead at night as well, when cold winds blow in over the warm sea. Sometimes, these clouds bring localized showers to coastal areas. Fogs too can form at sea in the same way, and creep a little way inland. At daybreak the sea is often shrouded in a thick mist which only disperses as the wind changes, or the sun's heat begins to dry it up. The overall effect of all this water is to make weather in coastal areas generally less extreme than farther inland. Because the sea retains heat well, nights tend to be warmer on the coast, with winters milder, and summers slightly cooler. Frosts are rare on sea coasts in the mid-latitudes.

Frequent battering by strong, prevailing westerly winds blowing in off the sea bends all the trees landwards

OUT FOR A BLOW
Seaside resorts can often be quite windy, as this postcard from the early 20th century acknowledges. Not only does the open sea provide no obstacle to winds blowing off the sea, but temperature differences between land and sea can generate stiff breezes.

CLEAR COAST
This picture shows the coast of Oregon in the northwest USA, but it is typical of west coasts everywhere in the mid-latitudes. Deep depressio are common at this latitude and here a cold front (pp. 34–35) has just passed over, moving inland. An overhang of cloud lingers in the upper air from the front itself, and cumulus clouds are still growing in its wal Further showers are clearly on their way. As the front moves inland, it may well produce progressively less rain, because there is less moistur available to feed its progress.

COASTAL FOG
Sea fog is an advection fog (pp. 48–49), which tends to persist until the direction of t wind changes, because the se is slow to heat up. Off the coa of Newfoundland in Canada (left), where warm westerly winds blow over a sea cooled by currents flowing down fro the Arctic, thick fogs can ling for days on end.

Growing cumulus clouds

Visibility tends to be good on coasts, partly because winds are stronger, but mainly because over the sea the air is much cleaner and there are far fewer small smoke and dust particles on which water can condense

ngering clouds
m cold front

ves begin to break in
llow water – where the
ter is less than twice as
p as the wave

Lack of "white horses" on the waves shows the wind is only light

WIND AND WAVES

The winds that help windsurfers skim across the surface of the sea may often be locally generated sea breezes. But the waves they ride may be created by winds thousands of kilometres away. Waves are whipped up by the wind when air turbulence over the water creates little pockets of low and high pressure that suck and push on the water. Just how big the waves are depends on the strength of the wind, how long it blows, and the "fetch" – that is, how far it blows over the water.

Warmer air from over the sea pushes cool air over the land downwards

Land cools quickly

Sea cools slowly

Nighttime land breeze

Sinking air over the land drives air seawards on the surface, creating a land breeze

Air rising over the warm sea pushes air at high altitude towards the land

Air pushed out to sea at high altitude increases the air pressure over the cool sea

sinks over
cool sea

Sinking air over the sea and rising air over the land drive sea air shorewards, creating a stiff sea breeze at the surface.

Air rises over the warm land about 1 km (1/2 mile) above the ground

Land warms up quickly in the sun

warms up
y slowly

Daytime sea breeze

Land and sea breezes

A marked characteristic of coastal areas is the frequent occurrence of local wind circulations called land and sea breezes. These are sporadic in mid-latitudes, but in the tropics they blow virtually every day. Both occur because land and water absorb and lose heat from the sun at different rates. During the day, the land heats far more quickly than the sea, and air begins to rise. As warm air rises above the land, cool air from the sea is drawn in underneath, creating a stiff sea breeze, blowing inland. At night, the situation is reversed. The land cools more quickly, and air begins to sink. The cool air pushes out under the warm air over the sea. This is called a land breeze.

Colours in the sky

PURE SUNLIGHT IS WHITE, but it is made up of the seven colours of the rainbow mixed together. As sunlight passes through the atmosphere, gases, dust, ice crystals, and water droplets in the air split it into its rich variety of colours. Clear skies look blue because gases in the air bounce mostly blue light towards our eyes. Sunset skies may be fiery red because the rays of the setting sun travel so far through the dense, lower atmosphere that nearly all but red is absorbed. But the endless stirring of the atmosphere by sun and wind constantly brings new colours to the sky. Sometimes, sunlight strikes ice and water in the air to create spectacular effects such as rainbows and triple suns.

Rainbows form in showery weather, when there is a break in the clouds after rain, and always appear on the opposite side of the sky to the sun. Occasionally, electrical discharges can bring dramatic colour to the sky – particularly at night.

THE COLOURS OF THE MOON
On rare occasions, raindrops may catch the reflection of bright moonlight to form a moonbow. The colours of the moonbow are faint but they are the same as those seen in a rainbow during the daytime.

POLAR LIGHTS
Occasionally, highly charged particles from the sun strike gases in the atmosphere high above the poles to create a spectacular display of coloured lights in the night sky. In the northern hemisphere, this is known as the *aurora borealis*; in the southern hemisphere, it is known as the *aurora australis*.

WRAPPED IN A RAINBOW
Rainbows seem to appear and disappear so miraculously that many cultures believe they have magical properties. To the Navajo Indians of southwest USA the rainbow is a spirit. The spirit is depicted on this blanket around two other supernatural beings, with a sacred maize, or corn, plant in the centre.

Low, stratus-type clouds in shadow

SAINTLY LIGHT
In thundery weather, sailors occasionally see a strange, glowing ball of light on the masthead. Called "St. Elmo's Fire", this is actually an electrical discharge, like lightning.

THREE SUNS AT ONCE
A colourful halo, or ring, around the sun is often seen in cirrostratus and, occasionally, high altostratus clouds. This phenomenon is caused by ice crystals in the cloud refracting, or bending, sunlight. Bright "mock suns", or sundogs, may also appear, with long, white tails pointing away from the left or right of the real sun.

MISTY GIANTS
The "Brocken Spectre" appears when sunlight projects the enlarged shadows of mountaineers onto low-lying mist or clouds nearby.

WATER COLOURS
Rainbows are simply the reflection of the sun in raindrops in the sky. They are curved because raindrops are round, and multi-coloured because each raindrop splits the sunlight into a spectrum of colours like a prism. As the sun catches each drop at a slightly different angle, a tiny part of the spectrum is reflected from each drop – some red, others yellow, and so on. The colours are always in the same order: red, orange, yellow, green, blue, indigo, and violet.

Rainbow is created by reflection from rain in a cloud much higher in the sky

Receding cumulonimbus cloud

Red on the top or outside of a "primary" rainbow

Yellow in the rainbow's centre

Violet on the bottom or inside of the rainbow

From aeroplanes, a rainbow can be seen as a full circle, because raindrops are round

Our changing weather

THE WORLD'S WEATHER has not always been the same. Since the Earth cooled and acquired its atmosphere some four billion years ago, its climate has gone through many changes, some lasting just a few years, others lasting hundreds of thousands of years. By far the most dramatic changes occur between cold periods (Ice Ages, or glacials), and warm periods (interglacials). In the last Ice Age, the weather was so cold that the polar ice sheets grew to cover a third of the Earth in ice over 240 m (790 ft) thick. We now live in an interglacial following the end of the last Ice Age, some 10,000 years ago. Since then, there have been many minor fluctuations in the weather. Now, many people believe humans are changing the atmosphere so much that the world is steadily warming up (global warming), endangering our very existence.

FOSSIL AIR
As tree sap solidified into amber long ago, creatures like this spider were trapped along with air bubbles. The air in amber could show what the Earth's atmosphere was once like, but it usually proves to be contaminated.

Close rings mean a cold year, far apart warm.

METEORIC FALL
Dinosaurs dominated the Earth for 250 million years, but they may have been killed off by a catastrophic change in climate. About 65 million years ago, a huge meteor may have struck the Earth, sending up so much dust that the sun's rays were blocked out, which made the Earth very cold.

PRESERVED IN ICE
Ice, drilled from glaciers, reveals what the climate was like when the ice formed. Tiny bubbles of air, frozen within the ice during the Ice Age, show that the atmosphere contained less carbon dioxide indicating that the greenhouse effect was less.

PAST WARMTH
The world's coal and oil deposits are the compressed remains of vast forests that grew in the Carboniferous, or coal-bearing, era. The climate of the Carboniferous era was much warmer than it is now.

GROWING EVIDENCE
Each ring in a cut tree trunk shows one year's growth. If the ring is wide, the tree grew well, and the weather was warm; if narrow, then it was cold.

WOOLLY TIM[E]
At the end of the last Ice Age, huge elephant-like creatures, called mammoths, roamed ne[ar] ice sheets far from the poles. They had hug[e] curling tusks and long, woolly coats to prot[ect] them from the cold. A few have been fou[nd] preserved, frozen almost intact, in Siber[ia].

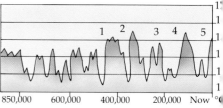

Years ago

850,000   600,000   400,000   200,000   Now °C

UPS AND DOWNS
Peaks in temperature over the past 850,000 years show five major warm interglacial periods (1–5 o[n] diagram), interspersed by five Ice Ages, when temperatures on Earth were 3°C (5°F) cooler tha[n] they are now – cold enough for vast ice sheets to extend half way through North America, as far a[s] the Alps in Europe, and over New Zealand.

VIKING VOYAGE
Around 1000–1200 A.D., the world's weather became so warm that much of the Arctic ice cap melted. At that time, Viking voyagers were sailing across the Atlantic, settling in Iceland and Greenland, and even reaching America. But the return of cold weather in the little Ice Age, from 1450 to 1850, brought back the ice sheets, and destroyed the Viking communities there.

WEATHER JOURNAL
Old diaries and weather records, kept by amateur meteorologists, are rich sources of past climates. Such diaries were particularly popular in 18th-century France and England. Among the best were those diaries kept by Thomas Barker in England between 1736 and 1798. His records give an almost complete record of over 60 years of weather.

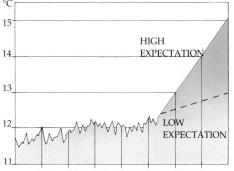

OLE IN THE SKY
zone is a bluish gas that occurs aturally in very small uantities high in the mosphere. It plays a vital le in protecting us from e sun's harmful traviolet radiation, that n cause skin cancer, and op plants growing. ecently, a hole has ppeared every Spring in the zone layer over the Antarctic shown in this satellite otograph – and levels of ozone in e atmosphere are declining. If this is not opped, the effect will be disastrous.

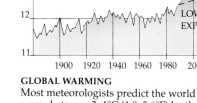

°C

GLOBAL WARMING
Most meteorologists predict the world will warm between 2–4°C (1.8–3.6°F) by the year 2030, unless we do something drastic to cut down the increase in greenhouse gases. Some estimates are more conservative.

HIGH EXPECTATION

LOW EXPECTATION

SATANIC MILLS
People's activities first began to affect the atmosphere with the increase in heavy industry in the early 19th century. Smoke from thousands of factory chimneys and soot from millions of coal fires in homes in vast, new cities created a real problem of smog (pp. 48–49) – as they still do in many parts of the world.

Climate in crisis
In recent years, people have become increasingly worried about the effects of human activities on the world's weather. Most meteorologists are now convinced that the world is getting warmer, due to increased "greenhouse" gases in the atmosphere – though just how much warmer they cannot agree. Greenhouse gases are beneficial in the right quantities. Like the panes of glass in a greenhouse, they trap heat and keep the Earth snug and warm, but now they are keeping the Earth too warm. Carbon dioxide is the main greenhouse gas, and most of the increase comes from burning coal, oil, and wood, but methane from rice fields and rubbish dumps, and CFCs from aerosol sprays and refrigerators also contribute to the greenhouse effect. If the Earth becomes just a few degrees warmer, polar ice will melt, drowning such low-lying cities as Sydney, London, and New York.

THE DEATH OF THE FOREST
ery year tropical forest the size of Iceland cut and burned to make temporary cattle sture – mostly in Brazil's Amazon Basin. eteorologists are uncertain exactly how s will affect the climate. Rainfall may drop fewer trees put less moisture into the air. e loss of trees may also increase the green-use effect. Trees are vital in absorbing cess carbon dioxide from the air as they ow – and add more as they burn.

THE CULPRIT
Car and lorry exhausts emit all kinds of pollutants, such as nitrous oxide and lead, and vast quantities of the greenhouse gas, carbon dioxide.

Home weather station

Pʀᴏꜰᴇssɪᴏɴᴀʟ ᴍᴇᴛᴇᴏʀᴏʟᴏɢɪsᴛs have a great deal of sophisticated equipment and thousands of weather stations to help them track the weather (pp. 12–13). But you can easily keep your own local weather watch with simple instruments – some of which can be made easily at home – and your own eyes. The longer the period over which observations are made, the more interesting and more valuable they become. But you must take measurements at exactly the same time at least once every day, without fail. This way your records can be more easily compared with those made by the professionals. The most important readings are rainfall, temperature range, wind speed and direction, and air pressure. If you can, record the humidity and soil temperature as well, and make a visual estimate of how much of the sky is covered by cloud.

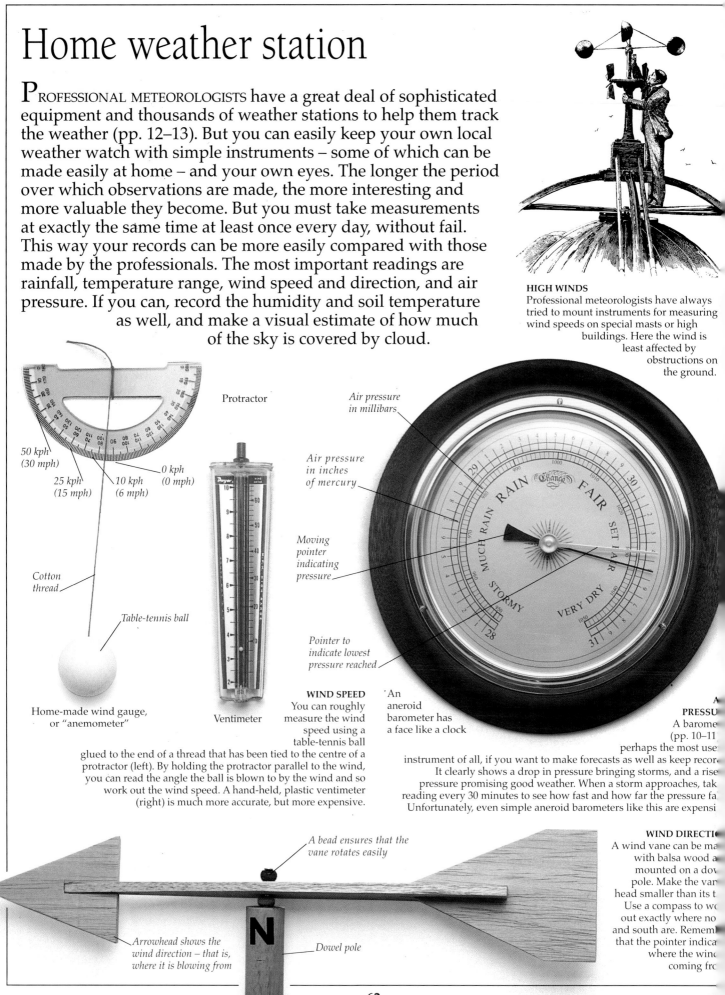

HIGH WINDS
Professional meteorologists have always tried to mount instruments for measuring wind speeds on special masts or high buildings. Here the wind is least affected by obstructions on the ground.

Protractor

50 kph (30 mph)

25 kph (15 mph)   10 kph (6 mph)   0 kph (0 mph)

Cotton thread

Table-tennis ball

Home-made wind gauge, or "anemometer"

Ventimeter

Air pressure in millibars

Air pressure in inches of mercury

Moving pointer indicating pressure

Pointer to indicate lowest pressure reached

WIND SPEED
You can roughly measure the wind speed using a table-tennis ball glued to the end of a thread that has been tied to the centre of a protractor (left). By holding the protractor parallel to the wind, you can read the angle the ball is blown to by the wind and so work out the wind speed. A hand-held, plastic ventimeter (right) is much more accurate, but more expensive.

An aneroid barometer has a face like a clock

A PRESSU
A barome (pp. 10–11 perhaps the most use instrument of all, if you want to make forecasts as well as keep recor
It clearly shows a drop in pressure bringing storms, and a rise pressure promising good weather. When a storm approaches, tak reading every 30 minutes to see how fast and how far the pressure fa Unfortunately, even simple aneroid barometers like this are expensi

A bead ensures that the vane rotates easily

WIND DIRECTI
A wind vane can be ma with balsa wood a mounted on a do pole. Make the var head smaller than its t Use a compass to wo out exactly where no and south are. Rememb that the pointer indica where the wind coming fro

Arrowhead shows the wind direction – that is, where it is blowing from

Dowel pole

CLOUD SNAPS

Photographs provide an accurate visual record of unusual weather conditions. It is important to make a note of the exact time and date when the picture was taken, and write it on the processed print.

SOIL TEMPERATURE

Special, right-angled thermometers are used to measure the temperature beneath the surface of the ground. Plants will survive if frost does not penetrate very deeply.

TEMPERATURE RANGE

A double-ended thermometer records the maximum and minimum temperatures reached each day. A magnet is used to reset the indicators every time a reading is taken. It is important to mount the thermometer out of direct sunlight – preferably in a box painted white, mounted a metre or so above the ground, and drilled with large holes for good ventilation.

WEATHER SKETCHES

Drawing clouds and other weather phenomena is a good way of learning to tell one type from another, and analyzing how they are formed.

SUN SCREENS

Professional weather instruments are kept inside ventilated shelters, known as Stevenson Screens. These protect them from direct sunlight, which could cause false results.

RAINFALL

A simple, plastic rain-gauge is quite accurate, provided you set it up securely at ground level in an exposed place. Each day take the measuring cylinder out to make a reading, empty it, and dry thoroughly. If you do not empty it, remember to subtract the previous day's measurement from your total each time.

Rain-gauge

...UMIDITY

...wet and dry hygrometer has two ...ermometers: the bulb of one is kept wet in ...stilled water and the other bulb dry. The ...fference in temperature between them indicates humidity on a scale provided by the makers. Only when the humidity is high can fog or clouds form.

...OME WIND OR RAIN ...

...eather records must be ...ken at the same time ...ch day, even if it is ...ining hard.

Measuring cylinder

KEEPING RECORDS

Record all instrument readings, along with the date and time, in a proper notebook divided into appropriate columns. Do not use a loose-leaf book, as pages could be lost.

Index

A B C

Acknowledgements

Dorling Kindersley would like to thank:
Robert Baldwin of the National Maritime Museum, Greenwich, for making instruments available for photography.
The Meteorological Office, Bracknell, for providing instruments for photography.
Met Check for the loan of instruments on pp. 62–63.
David Donkin for weather models on pp. 26, 34–33, 34–35, 44–45, and 53.
Sophie Mitchell for her help in the initial stages of the book.
Jane Parker for the index.

Picture credits

t=top b=bottom c=centre l=left r=right
Alison Anholt-White: 19, 28bc, 42cr
Aviation Picture Library: 20cl
Bridgeman Art Library: 17t, 42tl, 42bl, 43tr, 43br
British Antarctic Survey: 60c
Bruce Coleman Picture Library: 8cl, 14cr, 20c, 28tr, 28–29c, 29tl, 52b, 54bl, 54–55, 59tc
B. Cosgrove: 24–25, 24c, 24cr, 24bl, 25tr, 25cl, 28cl, 28c, 29tr, 29ctr, 29cr, 29cbr, 29br
Daily Telegraph Colour Library: 7tr, 43tc
Dr. E. K. Degginger: 46cl, 46cr, 47tr, 47c, 47b
E. T. Archive: 12c, 21br, 31br, 36tr
European Space Agency: 13tr
Mary Evans Picture Library: 10bc, 13bl, 20tl, 24tr, 30tl, 30bl, 37tr, 41br, 44tl, 45br, 46bl, 47tl, 48b, 53cr, 54cl, 60cl, 60cr

Werner Forman Archive: 18cl, 36bl, 38c, 58b, 61tl
Courtesy of Kate Fox: 22b
Hulton Deutsch Collection: 55br
Hutchison Library: 31bl, 61bl
Image Bank: 43cr, 56–57, 57tr
Istituto e Museo di Storia della Scienza (photos Franca Principe): 2br, 3bl, 10bl, 10r, 11tl, 11c, 11r, 11b
Landscape Only: 23cr
Frank Lane Picture Library: 20bl, 22tl, 30c, 36c, 41bl, 44bl
Mansell Collection: 18tl, 43cbl, 43cl
Meteorological Office: 12bl, 12br © Crown, 14cl, 15tl, 21t, 34t, 42tr, 45tl, 45tcl, 45c, 45tcr, 45tcr, 49bl
N.A.S.A.: 16tl
National Centre for Atmospheric Research: 13br, 37tc
N.H.P.A.: 44cl
R. K. Pilsbury: 8crt, 8crb, 15tc, 26–27, 32cl, 33tl, 33c, 34cl, 34bl, 35t, 50cl, 50c, 50cr, 51tc, 51tl, 51br

Planet Earth: 9cl, 18cr, 20br, 23cl, 41t, 53tr, 54br, 55bl, 56b
Popperfoto:21bl
Rex Features: 13tl
Ann Ronan Picture Library: 6tl, 12t, 13c, 14tl, 23bl, 27bl, 27br, 38tl, 61cr
Royal Meteorological Society: 28tl
David Sands: 25br
R.F. Saunders:20–21t
Scala: 11tc
Science Photo Library: 36-37, 40c, 40bl, 40bc, 58c, 58–59, 61cl
Frank Spooner/Gamma: 38bl
Stock Boston: 48c
Tony Stone Picture Library: 6bl, 18bl, 3 48–49, 52–53
Wildlife Matters: 8tr, 9tr
Zefa: 7cb, 7b, 24cl, 25tl, 39t, 47tc, 49br, 50bl, 61br

Illustrations by: Eugene Fleury, John Woodcock